INVESTING
IN ONE LESSON

INVESTING
IN ONE LESSON

MARK SKOUSEN

Since 1947
**REGNERY
PUBLISHING, INC.**
An Eagle Publishing Company • Washington, DC

Library of Congress Cataloging-in-Publication Data
Skousen, Mark.
Investing in one lesson / Mark Skousen.
p. cm.
Includes index.
ISBN 978-1-59698-522-3
1. Investments. 2. Portfolio management. 3. Stocks. 4. Securities. I. Title.
HG4521.S613 2007
332.6—dc22
2007019953

Published in the United States by
Regnery Publishing, Inc.
One Massachusetts Avenue, NW
Washington, DC 20001
www.regnery.com

Manufactured in the United States of America

10 9 8 7 6 5 4 3 2 1

Books are available in quantity for promotional or premium use. Write to Director of Special Sales, Regnery Publishing, Inc., One Massachusetts Avenue NW, Washington, DC 20001, for information on discounts and terms or call (202) 216-0600.

Dedicated to
ALEX GREEN

Investing in One Lesson is written for:

- Investors who want a quick understanding of how Wall Street works, and a simple, successful formula to build wealth in the stock market.

- Investors who feel frustrated trying to find profitable stocks and mutual funds, who often buy stocks when it's too late, or who have lost money repeatedly in the market.

- Businesspeople, professionals, and others who have been successful in their careers and need some useful techniques for making money without taking a college course in the stock market.

- Investors who are not happy with their money managers, or are worried that their money managers may go astray in the future.

- Busy people who have other interests besides investing and want an easy-to-follow method of making money in the markets, year after year, without losing sleep at night.

- Investors who are overwhelmed with too many investment choices and want an uncomplicated formula to make money.

If you fit into any of these categories, then *Investing in One Lesson* has the answers for you.

CONTENTS

"An investment in knowledge always pays the best interest."

BENJAMIN FRANKLIN

"In the land of the blind, the one-eyed is king."

OLD WALL STREET SAYING

"Gather ye rosebuds while ye may,
Old Time is still a-flying,
And this same flower that smiles today,
Tomorrow will be dying."

ROBERT HERRICK (1591-1674)

ONE

IS THIS YOUR STORY?

"Sell them and you'll be sorry,
Buy them and you'll regret,
Hold them and you'll worry,
Do nothing and you'll fret."

OLD SAYING ON WALL STREET

In 2005, I spoke before a large group of investors in New Orleans, not long after Hurricane Katrina had devastated the gulf region and destroyed the lives of hundreds of thousands of people. After my talk, a woman approached me and told me about the financial struggles she and her family faced in making ends meet following the massive storm. Despite a successful career in real estate and a consistent savings plan, she expressed grave doubts about her ability to understand Wall Street. She and her husband just couldn't seem to make any consistent profits in the stock market. They jumped in and out of markets, tried this and that formula, subscribed to this and that investment newsletter, watched financial TV shows, but nothing seemed to work. When Katrina struck New Orleans, they didn't have the funds to maintain their lifestyle or their children's education. They feared that they would never have enough for retirement or, heaven forbid, they'd be unprepared for another natural disaster.

In my talk, I had asked a series of questions, and this woman, like many in the audience, nodded her head in wondering the same things. I asked:

- Why do individuals who are successful in business and other careers often fail as investors?
- How is it that great companies with booming sales and earnings can see their stock price languish for years, while old, established firms in a shrinking industry can outperform the market as a whole?
- Why is good news for the economy sometimes bad news for the stock market, and vice versa? Why is it that a strong employment report can send the market sharply lower, while slower economic growth can spark a stock market rally?
- Why do markets sometimes move with such explosive force, with investors valuing a company at $100 a share one day and $130 a share—or $70 a share—the next?
- Finally, why is it that doctors, lawyers, and other professionals can provide accurate, valuable help consistently while most professional money managers can't keep up with the stock averages?

I sympathized with this woman and the rest of the audience because I've asked these same questions myself over the years. It was as if they were all asking the same question: "Can anyone make sense of this crazy world we call Wall Street?"

Clearly there is a huge gulf between the companies that make up the economy on the one hand, and the financial markets we call Wall Street on the other. But there is hope. This book aims to bridge this gulf in a clear, definitive fashion. Just as Oedipus solved the Riddle of the Sphinx, this book attempts to solve once and for all the puzzle of Wall Street by revealing in one lesson how you can become at the very least a good investor, and more likely a superior one. By mastering this lesson—and it is surprisingly easy to understand and apply—you will be a consistent winner on Wall Street. And you'll be able to sleep at night, pursue your other interests without worry, and build a fortune while you are young enough to enjoy it.

Let's get started.

The Deceptive Nature of Wall Street

Why is investing so frustrating? The crux of the lesson is simple but often ignored: *Wall Street is not Main Street.* In other words, the business of investing is *not* the same as investing in a business.

Once you understand this vital precept—and the easiest way to profit from it—you will be on the road to success. To thrive as an investor, you must first confront the beast called Wall Street in order to see what challenges you face. You must understand the workings of the stock market before you can grasp how to succeed. This is the purpose of the first half of this book—to unravel the mystery of how the stock market functions. The second section will describe a crucial part of the lesson—a simple strategy for successful investing based on the way the market really works. It's a formula that took me many years to work out through constant application of sound economic and financial principles, and through empirical studies that illuminated the best single path to wealth building. After completing the book, you will be ready to escape the Wall Street blues and start a new life of prosperous investing.

The day I started writing this book, two big events occurred on Wall Street: firstly, Yahoo, one of the world's largest technology companies, announced great news—earnings (profits) had jumped 83 percent in the most recent quarter. Yet, amazingly, investors shrugged off the revelation, and the share price immediately plunged 13 percent when the market opened. And secondly, Miramar Mining, a Canadian gold mining company, reported the same results it had been reporting for the past three years: absolutely zero revenues from its gold mine in Hope Bay, near the Arctic Circle in Canada. There was plenty of gold in the ground, yet the company remained at least a couple of years away from operating a mine. Furthermore, Miramar did not report any increase in its proven reserves. Surprisingly enough, however, the firm's shares had shot up 30 percent in the previous month.

How is this possible? Why is good news on Main Street often bad news on Wall Street, and vice versa? I wouldn't raise this issue if it were a bizarre or unique occurrence. Unfortunately, the financial marketplace is infused with this kind of apparent irrationality, and some observers think markets are becoming even more unpredictable.

Why is investing so puzzling and complicated? Answering this question is the first step to succeeding on Wall Street.

The famous British economist John Maynard Keynes, a seasoned speculator in stocks and commodities for half a century, once called the stock market a "game of Snap, of Old Maid, or Musical Chairs—a pastime in which he is victor who says 'Snap' neither too soon nor too late, who passes the Old Maid to his neighbor before the game is over, who secures a chair for himself when the music stops." This seemingly unpredictable "casino" of "animal spirits" is so maddeningly troublesome, Keynes concluded, that "it cannot be claimed as one of the outstanding triumphs of *laissez-faire* capitalism." Indeed, the uncertain, unstable, and perverse nature of the stock exchange can be baffling to part-time investors who have spent their lives working in a career outside Wall Street. I've met many people in all walks of life—physicians, dentists, sales people, manufacturers, artists, teachers—who have been successful in life, yet have failed miserably when it comes to investing. How can this be, and what can be done about it?

Are You Frustrated? I Have a Solution

Too many people become disappointed by losses in their first attempt at investing in stocks. Frustrated with their inability to make money, many of them simply abandon the stock market and seek out simpler, less risky investments like interest-bearing bank accounts, insurance products, and real estate. But stocks offer many advantages over these alternatives. By giving up on the stock market, investors miss out on some of the greatest opportunities to profit in the financial world. Offering a low-cost and time-saving method for building a solid nest egg, stocks belong in every investor's arsenal of wealth accumulation. But you must learn to invest in them correctly.

You may be overwhelmed by the vast array of investment choices these days: technology, biotech, commodities, junk bonds, IPOs, emerging markets, international markets, midcaps, growth or value plays—the list is practically endless. Then there are 9,000 mutual funds and 20,000 domestically traded stocks to choose from, dozens of brokerage firms to enlist, newsletters and magazines to subscribe to, and financial programs to watch on television. The options boggle the mind. But in this book, I will help you limit your choices to the very best ones.

"The Lesson," like many lessons in life, is not obvious, even to seasoned investors who think they've figured out how the stock market works. Just as a golf pro can sometimes blunder on the final hole and lose the tournament, so too can experienced traders overlook the lesson and lose a great deal of money. One thirty-year Wall Street veteran I know forgot the lesson and lost millions in the currency markets in less than a month, almost ending up bankrupt.

Applying this vital lesson will protect you from significant losses and help you to flourish in this most challenging marketplace. Ignoring it will dramatically increase your chances of suffering financial setbacks and even disaster. The lesson can be an expensive one if you have to discover it through the tough school of experience. But learn it early, and it will help those who are successful in their own careers to become profitable investors as well. Even seasoned investors will likely gain some valuable insights.

What is the lesson? It bears repeating: *Wall Street is not Main Street.* A stock is a unique entity; its price is affected by factors different from those that determine the value of an individual company. Remember: the business of investing is *not* the same as investing in a business.

My Background in Investing

Let me begin with a little personal background. I've been a financial economist, investor, and advisor since the 1970s. I made my first investment in the early 1960s, when I was taking a personal economics class at Sunset High School in Portland, Oregon. The teacher asked us to choose a stock from the financial pages, watch its daily movements, and determine the cause of its ups and downs. I chose a company I was familiar with, the grocery chain Safeway, where my mother shopped. I learned an important lesson during this class: some stocks don't move at all. Safeway remained virtually unchanged over a three-month period. Not a very exciting beginning for me on Wall Street.

Yet my choice of Safeway was symbolic of my search for financial success: Is there a "safe way" to make money?

Over the next several decades, I learned that Safeway's stock was an exception to the rule. Most stocks move a great deal, almost every day or every week. Short-term volatility and quarterly reporting are the watchwords of Wall Street. In the mid-1970s, I entered the marketplace full time as managing editor of *Personal Finance*, a monthly investment newsletter. Those were heady times when a budding financial revolution was introducing investors to nontraditional investments such as interest-bearing checking accounts, money market funds, "nothing down" real estate, and the "trinity" of gold, silver and Swiss francs, all at a time when traditional stock and bond markets were floundering. My first investment as a professional was not a stock or a bond, but a silver dollar!

I've witnessed tremendous volatility in my lifetime: bull markets, bear markets, manias, credit crunches, 21 percent interest rates and 1 percent interest rates, even a stock market crash or two. I celebrated my fortieth birthday on October 19, 1987, when the Dow plunged 22 percent in one day. I've also invested in practically every vehicle imaginable: stocks, bonds, mutual funds, real estate, foreign markets, penny stocks, gold, silver, futures, options, and hedge funds. I've written columns and guest articles for numerous publications, including the *Wall Street Journal, Forbes*, my own newsletter *Forecasts & Strategies*, and an e-letter for Investment U. Relying on my background and expertise in "Austrian" economics (I'm one of only a handful of financial economists who use the business cycle model of Ludwig von Mises and Friedrich Hayek), I've made some good predictions, as well as a few blunders. I've made money, even a million dollars on one trade, and I've suffered losses from time to time. Through it all, I've managed to build a substantial portfolio that will allow my wife and I to enjoy a comfortable early retirement.

What Is the Secret to Financial Success?

Throughout these years of investing and investigating, I have often been approached by attendees at investment conferences who are searching for the secret to financial success. Oftentimes they will ask me, "If you could identify one lesson of investing, what would it be?"

It's a tall order, even for someone who has had decades of experience on Wall Street with some success. I've pondered that question time and again as I have lived through the ups and downs of the markets. No doubt there are many vital lessons, but the more I thought about it, the more I wondered if my entire investment philosophy could be summed up in a single lesson. The hunt has been an exciting adventure, and now, after all these years, I think I've found the answer.

Two

WHAT'S YOUR BUSINESS?

"There is nothing like losing all you have in the world for teaching
you what not to do. And when you learn what not to do in order
not to lose money, you begin to learn what to do in order to win.
Did you get that? You begin to learn!"

EDWIN LEFÈVRE, *REMINISCENCES OF A STOCK OPERATOR* (1923)

This chapter involves a valuable exercise: comparing the two worlds
of business and investing. Let me begin with a story. While sleeping in
a hotel room in Los Angeles, where I was scheduled to speak at an
investment conference, I was awakened early one morning by the loud
ringing of the telephone. I lifted the receiver and heard from a man who
said he was a new subscriber to my newsletter service. His voice was
intense and emotional. He said he was worried about an investment he
had made in a "no load" offshore commodity fund that had "guaranteed" 25 percent annualized returns. He had been investing in this offshore fund for a few years, and at first his account records showed
substantial profits, just as the fund manager had promised. Then he
asked for the return of some of his funds, and that's when the trouble
began.

"For three months, I asked for my money, but never received a
check. Finally, I received a check, but it bounced." In a panicky voice,
he asked, "What should I do? Have I lost it all?"

I thought for a moment, and then delivered the bad news. "I'm afraid your 'no load' fund has become an 'all load' fund," I said gently. "You are most likely out of luck, and the investment account is probably a fraud. You have probably lost everything."

There was an awkward silence on the other end of the telephone. Finally, I asked, "How much did you invest?"

His answer floored me. "Half a million dollars—my entire retirement," he said despondently. Then he added another shocker: "And I invested my wife's money, too—a quarter of a million dollars."

I couldn't believe it. This man's entire retirement fund—and his wife's—representing a lifetime of savings and hard work, had suddenly disappeared down the drain, all because of a single stupid decision.

After another long moment of silence, I asked him about his background. He was a retired doctor who had had a successful medical practice for many years. What an irony! Here was a man who had spent years training to become a physician, then ran a successful medical business for his adult life, and suddenly when he retired, decided to risk his entire retirement plan in a dubious investment scheme.

Unfortunately, the doctor's experience was not as rare as you might think. In several recent articles, the *Wall Street Journal* has related the stories of numerous retirees who lost their fortunes after they sold their lifetime businesses and became investors. I asked myself, "Why is it that some of the most successful people in business and life can be failures on Wall Street?"

If this retired doctor had understood the business of investing as well as he understands the practice of medicine, I thought, perhaps he would have avoided this tragic mistake. He surely has learned all the unique principles that pertain to medicine, but he doesn't understand that there are also distinctive rules of investing that don't always apply to other professions and activities. Perhaps it's good medicine for a doctor to invest all his efforts in one form of treatment for an ill patient. But when investing money, you never want to put all your investment eggs in one nest. In short, the doctor failed to understand the unique business of investing.

The distraught doctor wanted my advice. I told him to contact the authorities and try to get his money back, but the chances were slim because the funds were outside the country. The government bails out a lot of businesses, but when it comes to individual investors, they're often just out of luck. The doctor would likely have to start from scratch and rebuild his financial life the old-fashioned way: by living frugally, saving regularly, and educating himself about the business of investing. It would be painful, but he could do it, I said. I quoted from Edwin Lefèvre's classic book, *Reminiscences of a Stock Operator*, the apocryphal tale of legendary speculator Jesse Livermore, who said, "Losing it all is the beginning of learning." Livermore also observed, ironically in this case, "The training of a stock trader is like a medical education." Yet I suspect it was little consolation. I wished the doctor luck and hung up the telephone.

A Million Stock Market Stories in the Naked City

I hope you've never made the mistake our doctor friend committed. But large numbers—I'd say a majority—of people have undoubtedly invested in a stock that promised the world but delivered only headaches and sleepless nights—stocks that fell 50 percent, 70 percent, or even 90 percent after buying them.

Years ago in my newsletter, I recommended a tech stock that was selling at around $1 a share, suggesting that if everything went right, the stock could be a "ten bagger," meaning that subscribers could make 1,000 percent on their money in a few years. Now understand that I don't recommend these speculative positions very often and when I do, I warn subscribers that they should use only a small portion of their portfolio and not go overboard. Most speculations of this type never live up to their potential, but fortunately this one did, rising to $13 a share

within a few years. I was elated and thought my subscribers would cel-
ebrate with me. But I was sadly mistaken. It turns out that the majority
didn't get on board until the stock had already risen by double digits, to
$10 a share or higher. And when the stock fell back down to earth—
dropping from $13 a share to under $3—I began hearing the com-
plaints.

One subscriber was so upset that he called me on the telephone. He
was one of those who waited too long, bought late, and now had a losing position. He also apparently got greedy and bought too much of the
stock, ignoring my advice to put no more than 10 percent of one's portfolio in any single investment. He told me that his wife was so distraught
that she had been crying for three hours. Three hours!

Investing can be an emotional business. I'm reminded of a remark
by Lord Overstone: "No warning can save a people determined to grow
suddenly rich."

The Challenge of Wall Street

Becoming financially independent by investing in the stock market,
mutual funds, or real estate is not an easy task. Most investors are not
suited to the rigors of market discipline. As a collector of investment
books, I'm reminded often by their titles how intimidating investing can
be:

> *Why Most Investors Are Mostly Wrong Most of the Time*, by
>   William X. Scheinman
> *Why the Best-Laid Investment Plans Usually Go Wrong*, by
>   Harry Browne
> *Wiped Out: How I Lost a Fortune in the Stock Market While the
>   Averages Were Making New Highs*, by "Anonymous Investor"
> *Investment Policy: How to Win the Loser's Game*, by Charles Ellis
> *Wall Street: the Other Las Vegas*, by Nicolas Darvas

I recall a comment once made about the investing public by Peter Lynch, who ran the Fidelity Magellan Fund, the most successful mutual fund in the 1970s and 1980s. He noted that despite the fund's huge success, the majority of shareholders lost money! Why? Because they tried to time the market and never stayed fully invested throughout the period Lynch ran the fund. Whenever the market fell, they would panic, get out, and then try to get back in after the price turned around. They were always chasing the price, and it never worked out.

Recent studies confirm Peter Lynch's story. Over the past twenty years, the average stock-market mutual fund gained 13 percent a year compounded, but the average fund investor earned only 3.5 percent. This is because most investors didn't buy and hold. Instead, they tried to pick the tops and bottoms of the fund's value—and failed. Why? Because many of them misunderstood the basic principles that govern stock prices. When the largest companies are posting big profits or the economy is in a general upswing, they think this will automatically translate into a rising stock market. That's good common sense—but common sense does not move stock prices.

The stock market is much more perverse than that, which makes it incredibly hard to understand and even more difficult to predict. Even among the wealthy elite, few have made it big as stock market traders. Take a look at the annual *Forbes* list of the 400 richest Americans. How many billionaires made the list by investing in the stock market? A very small percentage—less than 10 percent, according to my calculations. And even among these ultra-successful investors were many professional money managers who made their millions through fees rather than by picking good stocks for their own portfolios. The reality is that the most popular road to riches was not the stock market, mutual funds, or even real estate. In fact, it was not investing at all. Whether they were involved in manufacturing, retail stores, banking, insurance, computers, or managing other people's money, the *Forbes* Richest 400 made their fortunes primarily through creating and expanding their own businesses.

Does it surprise you that stockbrokers often have a better year than their customers? That floor traders on the New York Stock Exchange beat the market? That managers of mutual funds do better in their individual portfolios? That real estate brokers are often the most successful investors in the property business? That coin dealers usually make more money in trading coins than you do in investing in them? Or that company officers profit the most from a stock's initial public offering? That's because investing is their business and they usually understand that the normal rules of other kinds of business don't always apply to it.

The difficulties facing individual investors remind me of a classic book in finance, *Where Are the Customers' Yachts?*, by Fred Schwed Jr. Schwed describes the disparity between jet-setting Wall Street bankers, brokers, traders, and analysts on one side, and their hapless customers on the other. He tells the story of a visitor to New York who admired the yachts that the bankers and brokers had in the harbor. Naïvely, he asked where the customers' yachts were. Naturally, there were no customers' yachts. Schwed's cynical book was published in 1940, but his "good hard look at Wall Street" is just as relevant today. To be fair, there are customers' yachts—many of them—but there could be a lot more if investors better understood the business of high finance.

How About a Professional Money Manager?

Investors who fear the market often seek out money managers to take over their portfolios. They've heard tales of professionals who have made 100 percent or more a year in hedge funds or other exotic managed accounts. Of course, some money managers really do succeed, but here again there are no guarantees. Studies have shown that the vast majority of professional money managers can't beat the market, and many of them lose money for their clients. And then, because clients tend to develop a friendship with their money manager or stock broker, it becomes difficult to take their money elsewhere. In sum, finding a professional money manager can be helpful, but it is no panacea for the stock market blues.

Advice to the Busy Executive

I'm not suggesting that you must become a stockbroker, coin dealer, or real estate developer to be successful in the investment world. Nor am I urging you to drop all your outside interests and hobbies to concentrate only on investing. You don't have to treat your portfolio like a full-time business in order to make a decent profit. In fact, part of the lesson includes a very simple strategy—a shortcut, if you will—that will keep you out of trouble and help your portfolio grow without devoting your life to investing.

Education is important. Why have you been successful in your business and able to accumulate surplus funds? Because you concentrated on doing things right. You took the necessary time to educate yourself, to research ways to become more proficient in your job or business. You earned a degree. You got involved. You relied on the expertise of others, and did your homework. Most of all, you learned which strategies work and which don't in your particular industry.

That's the same attitude you need when it comes to investing. You need to understand the basics of the stock market before you can proceed. You can make money in stocks, real estate, collectibles—choose your passion—but only if you take the time and spend the money necessary to learn what it's all about. Tragically, all too often an investor "will risk half his fortune in the stock market with less reflection than he devotes to the selection of a medium-priced automobile," to quote Edwin Lefèvre.

In this chapter, I have attempted to describe the differences between Wall Street and Main Street, between the world of investing and the world of business. In the next chapter, I go into more detail on how the stock market often gets separated from its fundamental business purpose.

Three

A ROCKY MARRIAGE

"There is nothing so disastrous as a rational investment policy in an irrational world."

JOHN MAYNARD KEYNES

"It may come as a shock to the thinking man to be told that billions of dollars of trades on the stock market are executed without reference to any definable standard of value."

ARNOLD BERNARD, FOUNDER, VALUE LINE INVESTMENT SURVEY

What kind of business is Wall Street? This chapter will help you see that a publicly traded stock is quite distinct from a private business. *The business of investing is not the same as investing in a business.*

You've read that sentence before. It is *the* vital lesson for understanding and achieving success in the stock market. In fact, by not recognizing the difference between the "business of investing" and "investing in a business," you could end up with a lot of bad investments. Or worse, like the medical doctor mentioned previously, your hard-earned wealth could be wiped out or severely reduced by making the wrong investment choice.

The key point is that a company and its stock are two separate things—closely related, and usually having the same goals, but often going in different directions. Like a marriage, they are sometimes at odds with each other.

Now I'm sure you've read books or heard speeches by Warren Buffett and Peter Lynch instructing you to "treat investing like a business" or "invest in a real and ongoing profitable business," implying that's all there is to it. Buffett is famous for saying, "I buy companies, not stocks." Unfortunately, it's not that simple. If it were, everyone would be as successful as Buffett.

In reality, you cannot simply use the typical business evaluation method to buy good stocks because the stock market is not a typical business. It is a very unique business, unlike any other, as I will demonstrate. If all you needed were standard accounting yardsticks to determine good and bad companies, investing would be straightforward and easy. However, in the financial markets you will encounter many other forces that push stock prices in the opposite direction of the business fundamentals and lead you astray, much to the detriment of your wealth and future retirement. In fact, I would even say that taking a company public through the stock exchange is a surefire way to cause a separation in the marriage between a company and its shareholders.

A publicly traded company is inherently a rocky marriage between the company and its shareholders. Often it results in a "separation" between the company's intrinsic value and its stock price. But this is not a "divorce," for stock prices ultimately return to their intrinsic value. Mathematicians and economists call it "regression to the mean." Yet the time it takes for a reconciliation is unpredictable. It could be months or even years before the company value and stock price get back together. In this chapter, I explain why.

The Tale of Two Stocks

Here's an example of why investing in the stock market is different from investing in a business. Suppose you follow the advice of Warren Buffett or his teacher, Ben Graham, and decide to invest in a publicly traded company with a superior business model. You read the financial news and consider investing in Yahoo, a blue-chip technology company. You do a little further investigating and discover that the company is doing extremely well. Sales are climbing, new deals are being made around the world, and profits are soaring. If you wanted to own part of a business, could you find a better opportunity than this rapidly growing tech company?

You remember reading all sorts of books by financial historians informing you that in the long run stock prices are driven by earnings (profitability). Yahoo is highly profitable, and there is every indication that it will remain so in the future. The stock price has been rising and is in a clear upward trend. All indications show that the company is a great investment.

So now you have done your homework, and you are ready to invest. Confidently, you call your broker or go to his Internet website and buy 1,000 shares of Yahoo, which trades actively on the Nasdaq.

The next day the stock drops 13 percent on heavy volume.

You think I'm joking? Not at all. It happens all too frequently on Wall Street. Sometimes good companies lose up to half their value in short order. In fact, the 13 percent one-day drop happened to Yahoo the day I began writing this book, as noted in Chapter One. On that day, Yahoo announced a 39 percent increase in revenue growth, and an 83 percent rise in profits to $1.7 billion. It had $2.5 billion in cash, with aggressive expansion plans. The stock had risen 20 percent in the previous few months. Everything looked great. But because it missed its earnings target by a penny a share — one penny! — investors and institutions dumped the stock.

The company did not even post a loss, mind you; it recorded a large gain that wasn't quite as much as promised. Imagine missing a positive earnings target by *one penny* and witnessing your stock collapse by 13 percent. Could any investor have predicted such an outcome?

Now, before you start to think that Wall Street can only deliver doom to your finances, recall our counterexample of Miramar Mining, which owns major mining properties near the Arctic Circle. It expects to extract primarily gold from the Hope Bay Mine in the "near future." But so far, Miramar has not made a single dollar of revenue nor has it produced a single ounce of metal from its mines. It has no revenues from mining, only costs. Last year it lost $15 million, and had to raise an additional $15 million from investors to keep its operations going. Miramar is a far cry from achieving anywhere near the profitability of Yahoo. And yet, Miramar's market capitalization is $1 billion, and its stock shot up 50 percent in the past six months.

Neither Yahoo nor Miramar is an exception to the rule. In fact, this sort of thing happens with amazing regularity on Wall Street. Most publicly traded stocks move up and down unpredictably, while the underlying business behind the stock is constantly making progress, changing little from day to day.

Why do we witness what appears to be an irrational, fickle, manic-depressive mood on Wall Street? We'll find out in the next chapter.

Four

A PECULIAR INSTITUTION

"Corporation treasurers sleep soundly while stockholders walk the floor."

BEN GRAHAM

"The stock market and the economy are two different things."

MILTON FRIEDMAN

To understand how a highly successful company can see its stock temporarily collapse, or a losing company can see its stock soar, you must understand how the stock market develops and functions.

First of all, a stock is not the same as a company business. It is not simply "part ownership in a business," as Peter Lynch defines it. Yes, a stock certificate means you are one of the owners of a business with shareholder rights, but you in fact only have a marginal influence on the company. It is not the same as working for the firm or serving on the board of directors. Yahoo's market capitalization fell by 13 percent in one day, yet the company continued to operate the same as it did the day before the stock dropped. The work activities of the company executives, employees, suppliers, and customers did not change one iota. The same applies to the money-losing mining company whose stock soared. Its workers are still hard at work building the mines in Argentina, Mexico and Peru. Regardless of whether the stock price goes up or down, everything is the same for the employees, the suppliers, and the customers. The change in stock price has affected the shareholders, but not the business itself.

In short, on Wall Street the value of a business may not change in the short run, even though the stock price changes every day, and sometimes radically.

The Stock Market and the Economy

Similarly, we can show that Wall Street and the overall economy do not always move together. The following chart indicates the difference between the stock market (as measured by the S&P 500 Index) and the economy (as measured by GDP growth) in the recent past.

Figure 1. **S&P 500 TOTAL RETURN AND REAL GDP, 1990–2007**

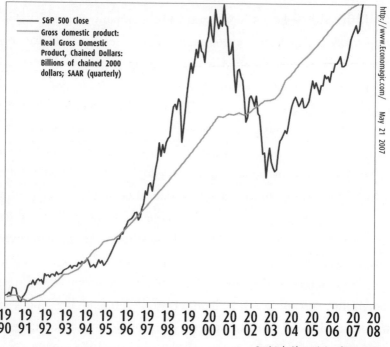

As you see from the graph, the stock market and the economy tend to move together over the long run, but there can be periods lasting years when the stock market outperforms real GDP growth, as well as times when it underperforms. For example, in the 1920s, real GDP increased at a 4 percent annualized rate, while the stock market index grew at a 20 percent rate—until 1929 and the subsequent bear market during the Great Depression. Similarly, in the 1990s, real GDP grew at a 4 percent rate, while the stock market increased at an average rate of 20 percent. By March 2000, at the height of the bull market, the value of stocks trading on the New York Stock Exchange exceeded 190 percent of America's GDP. During this time, Warren Buffett correctly warned that the U.S. market was vastly overvalued. And Robert Shiller, an economics professor at Yale University, published his bestseller, *Irrational Exuberance*, displaying a chart of the S&P 500 Index at a point "far higher than the historical average" and predicting that stocks would likely decline sharply. Then, as a bear market developed during the first years of the twenty-first century, stocks failed to keep up with the economy's annualized GDP growth rate of 3 percent.

The late 1990s is an excellent example of how Main Street and Wall Street can become extremely disconnected. In 1999, near the top of the Internet bubble, Amazon.com, the online book seller, had a market value of over $30 billion, ten times the combined market value of Barnes & Noble and Borders, its two brick-and-mortar competitors. And eToys, an online toy retailer, had a market value more than double the value of Toys "R" Us, which owned over 1,600 stores.

How a Company Goes Public

This chapter explains why the stock market and the country's economic performance often go separate ways. To understand the business of investing, we must begin by discussing how companies go public. Let's start with the step-by-step process of a company raising working capital by issuing stock. This is a process that every company listed on any stock exchange has had to endure. All securities were new issues once!

Yahoo serves as a perfect example. The company started out as a study hobby in the trailer of its founders, David Filo and Jerry Yang, who were Ph.D. students in electrical engineering at Stanford University. They created a list of their favorite Internet links that eventually became a website clearinghouse featuring a directory of other sites. It was named "Yahoo," based on the word's definition by Jonathan Swift to mean "rude, unsophisticated, [and] uncouth."

Before long, hundreds of people were accessing their guide. Word spread from friends to what quickly became a significant, loyal audience throughout the close-knit Internet community. Yahoo celebrated its first million-hit day in the fall of 1994, translating to almost 100,000 unique visitors.

At this point, based on growing traffic, the founders realized that they had a potential business on their hands. To expand their website into a full-fledged business, they needed additional capital. How could they raise the necessary funds? There are five traditional sources:

1. Use one's own capital or savings.
2. Borrow money from close friends and relatives.
3. Borrow money from banks and other financial institutions.
4. Issue bonds, i.e., short-term or long-term debt obligations that require you to pay interest every six months.
5. Sell shares of the company to the public.

Filo and Yang decided on the last alternative. In March 1995, the pair incorporated the business and met with dozens of Silicon Valley venture capitalists. Stock certificates were issued indicating ownership of the private company. By inviting others to invest in Yahoo, the founders had to give up some of their own ownership of the company. As part of the incorporation, the founders and other stockholders elected representatives (i.e., a board of directors) to meet regularly, oversee the company's operation, and issue annual reports on the company's progress. Eventually, they came across Sequoia Capital, a well-regarded firm whose most successful investments included Apple Computer, Atari, Oracle, and Cisco Systems. It agreed to fund Yahoo in April 1995 with an initial investment of nearly $2 million.

Realizing their new company had the potential to grow quickly, Filo and Yang began to shop for a management team. They hired Tim Koogle, a veteran of Motorola and an alumnus of the Stanford engineering department, as chief executive officer and Jeffrey Mallett, founder of Novell's WordPerfect consumer division, as chief operating officer. They secured a second round of funding in Fall 1995 from investors Reuters Ltd. and Softbank.

From Privately Held Stock to a New Issue (IPO)

Finally, to raise millions more in investment capital, Yahoo decided to go public—that is, to issue stock that would trade on an official exchange. Thousands of companies never take this step. They remain privately held, meaning that the company is owned by private individuals and the stock is not traded on a formal exchange. As a privately held company, the only way a stockholder can get his money back is to sell the stock privately to another shareholder or interested investor. Even then, he may get more or less than his original investment, depending on the value and outlook for the company.

Companies choose not to go public for a variety of reasons. Some entrepreneurs and business owners like to work without the strain of the public eye, the excessive regulations of the federal and state securities agencies, or pressure from public shareholders.

Most rapidly growing companies, however, find the benefits of "going public" outweigh the disadvantages. They especially like the ability to sell stock in the company on a formal exchange without much hassle.

Private companies are highly illiquid, meaning they have difficulty quickly raising cash, and going public often allows owners to sell out at a high price. Typically, a company does not go public until it has proven that it has a viable product and needs money for expansion. (Exceptions include firms that require substantial capital investment and lead times before production begins, such as Miramar Mining.)

Taking a new stock public is an art. The investment banker must decide how much stock to issue, at what price, and when to sell it to investors. Setting the right price for a new issue, called the initial public offering (IPO), is extremely important. If the price is considered too high, it is likely that the brokers won't be able to sell the entire issue, and it may be withdrawn. An excessively high-priced IPO will typically sell at a discount, that is, below the IPO price, which will irritate the first shareholders.

On the other hand, if the IPO price is too low, the stock becomes a hot issue, the entire issue sells out, and the stock sells at a premium. A small premium can be a healthy sign of interest in an IPO. But if the premium grows disproportionately large—like double or triple the IPO price—then brokers are forced to ration the hot issue to their favored customers, which can create ill will. Moreover, the company ends up giving a windfall to speculators who buy the new issue and sell it in the secondary market for a quick profit. The extra money could have gone to the company.

Bull markets, or rising markets, are the most favorable environment for new issues. More IPOs come out during this time than any other. The worst time to promote a new issue is during or right after a crash. Bad timing can ruin the prospects for a new issue even though the company is fundamentally sound. Moreover, IPOs are expensive and time consuming. It may take a year or two to get registered with the government (the Securities & Exchange Commission or other regulatory body) and the individual states, and the legal costs can be prohibitive for small companies. Many companies go public in Canada,

Europe, or other parts of the world to save on expenses and excessive regulations.

In April 1996, Yahoo's underwriter—an intermediary that helps to manage an IPO—decided to issue 26 million shares at $23 each, for an initial public offering that raised $338 million. The IPO was a success— the stock price immediately rose to a premium above its IPO price, but not so high as to enrich speculators and insiders at the expense of ordinary investors.

Beware of the "Burning Match"

If you are tempted to buy a new issue or IPO, consider the burning match analogy. I've used this example many times in my courses on investing. I start by lighting a match in front of students. I tell them that lighting the match is similar to a business deciding to go public. Then I pass along the burning match to a student, which is not unlike the next step in which the underwriter prepares the prospectus. The student quickly passes along the burning match to the next student, which is likened to the brokers and dealers who sell the offering to the public. The burning match is passed along to other students, and all the while the match is getting shorter and shorter until somebody gets burned. New issues are often much like the burning match. The company insiders make money, the underwriters and investment bankers get their share, the broker/dealers earn their commissions, and the preferred customers get a piece of the action. But once all these associates get their cut, the public investor often gets left holding the short match.

The ABCs of the Stock Exchange

After a company issues its new securities and qualifies as a listing on an exchange, investors begin buying and selling the stock on the secondary market. Literally thousands of stocks trade on official exchanges around the world, whether in New York, London, Paris, Amsterdam, or Tokyo, or electronically on the Nasdaq. These exchanges offer up-to-the-second bid-ask prices by computer to thousands of broker/dealers around the world. When the exchanges are open, stocks trade like a continuous auction.

The New York Stock Exchange, located at Broad and Wall Streets in Manhattan, is the oldest and largest stock market in the world. Founded in 1792, it started out with bond brokers meeting under a buttonwood tree between Broad and Wall Streets. Soon they began meeting in the Tontine Coffee House where memberships were called "seats." In 1817, it took the name New York Stock Exchange Board. A new building was constructed at the turn of the twentieth century. Today the Big Board is responsible for the highest dollar volume of securities traded in the United States. To be listed on the NYSE, a company must demonstrate profitability, high tangible assets, and broad ownership by the public. The exchange is noted for its specialists—members who serve a valuable function by acting as both brokers and dealers. These specialists are required to buy and sell shares of their assigned stocks at all times in order to keep an orderly market. To maintain liquidity, the specialists require investors to demonstrate adequate capital and reserves.

From a Private Firm to a Publicly Traded Company

Once Yahoo is given a stock symbol (YHOO) and begins trading on one or more stock exchanges, it is a publicly traded company. In Yahoo's case, it trades on the Nasdaq, not the New York Stock Exchange. The Nasdaq—originally an acronym for National Association of Securities Dealers Automated Quotations system—is an electronic trading market. It was founded in 1971 by the National Association of Securities Dealers (NASD), which divested it in a series of sales in 2000 and 2001. It is now owned and operated by The Nasdaq Stock Market, Inc. (symbol NDAQ), which went public in 2002. Listing around 3,200 companies, the Nasdaq usually has the highest daily trading volume of any U.S. market.

After going public, Yahoo is a different animal than it was as a private company. This may not seem like the case, however—it still needs to expand its website, control its costs, build a new facility, and increase its profits, just like a private firm. Nothing has changed from a business perspective. In fact, if the company had gone to a commercial bank or issued bonds, the lion's share of the new funds would have been invested in the business itself. But that's not necessarily the case when a private company goes public. With a new stock issue, a large number of the new shares go into the pockets of company officials, investment bankers, and underwriters who may wish to sell some or all of their shares on the secondary market for a profit. The founder/entrepreneur may even think it's time to cash in after years of hard work and invest the funds elsewhere.

Because Yahoo has gone public, the value of the business is suddenly exposed to the vicissitudes of the marketplace—the emotional decision-making of not only thousands of shareholders, but traders who may want to play this new listing, either on the long side or the short side. Instantly Yahoo becomes more volatile and can be worth much more or much less than its IPO price or even its "book value," as defined by accountants. Book value is the total value of the company's assets that shareholders would theoretically receive if a company were liquidated. But market capitalization can be substantially more or less than the book value, thus immediately making the firm (by going public) overvalued or undervalued.

Suddenly, with a publicly traded company, price and value are no longer the same. The money game on Wall Street is no longer the company business on Main Street. And that fact can lead to some rather perverse effects, as we will see in the next chapter.

Five

THE PERVERSITY OF "MR. MARKET"

"It is the emotional, nonprofessional investor who sends the price of a stock up or down in sharp, sporadic, and more or less short-lived spurts. A politician's speech, an ivory-tower pundit's pronouncement or prophecies, a newspaper item or a whispered rumor—such things are enough to trigger wildly enthusiastic buying sprees or hysterical orgies of panicky selling by thousands of self-styled investors."

J. PAUL GETTY, *HOW TO BE RICH*

"If all the deviltry of all the crooked stock market riggers of all time were raised to the hundredth power, it would count as nothing compared to the dissolution wrought by deluded crowds of investors whose imagination knows no discipline."

ARNOLD BERNHARD, FOUNDER OF VALUE LINE

The combined impact of the fickle speculator, the rank amateur, and even the seasoned trader can cause the stock of a fundamentally sound company to plummet in price, or a worthless penny stock to skyrocket. Fortunately, there is good news for the investor who knows "The Lesson." The patient, seasoned investor can profit immensely from these seemingly illogical turns in the market by avoiding overvalued plays and identifying truly undervalued opportunities as they come along.

With a publicly traded company, the "market" valuation is often quite different from the "business," or "book," valuation. The difference between the two values can last for years. Sometimes a company can sell for more than 50 percent above its book value. At other times, it can sell for less than book value. A stock price is determined by the perceived value placed on it by the shareholders who "vote" on the share price each day by buying or selling the stock. Benjamin Graham was famous for saying: "In the short run, the market is a voting machine; in the long run, it's a weighing machine."

Why does this disparity exist? The measure of a private business's net worth is set by rigorous and objective accounting rules. There's only *one* fixed value to worry about, set with each quarterly financial statement. But in the marketplace, the value of a publicly traded company is determined daily by thousands of investors deciding how much the company is worth to them—a perceived value that fluctuates constantly and may be subject to wild mood swings from optimism to pessimism and back.

The Stock Market as a Gigantic Auction House

In short, taking a company public on the stock exchange creates a very different creature than its fundamental business purpose. In the financial marketplace, the *entire* company is on sale every day and every minute the stock exchange is open. A publicly traded company is subject to a continuous auction of its shares and is thereby subject to "auction fever," when bidders get caught up in the emotions and excitement of the event and push a stock price way above its normal market value.

Here then is the *summa bonum* of this entire book and the primary lesson of investing. The stock exchange and the economy are two different things, loosely related in the long term, yet often going their separate ways in the short run. It's like a rocky marriage in a trial separation. The stock market is far more risky and volatile than business ventures, thus offering greater profit potential and at the same time a greater chance of losing your shirt.

A private company that does not trade on the stock exchange is highly illiquid and is not usually subject to "auction fever." It can be sold, but it is a lengthy, complex process that can't be done in a day or even a month. But once a company goes public on a major exchange, a part of the company can and does change ownership hands every day. If there are several thousand shareholders who own Yahoo, theoretically every single shareholder could call his broker today and sell the stock, or try to buy more. Company owners and executives can sell; employees can sell; shareholders can sell; and speculators can sell short—a trade in which an investor sells a stock he doesn't actually own. Their ability to sell or buy will be a function of the stock's liquidity, i.e., how many shares on average trade each day. Of course, not every shareholder is likely to sell his entire holdings at once. Only a minority of shareholders buy or sell stock each day, but it is conceivable that a day might come when there are thousands of sellers and few buyers, precipitating a stock market crash.

Stock trading volume—the number of shares trading each day—is on the rise. Gone are the days when stock certificates were stored in an investor's safe deposit box, held until death or an emergency. Moreover, access to the market is easier, with telephone and web trading available from anywhere in the world. But note that brokerage firms are not equipped to handle massive calls or online orders during a panic—in such an event, be prepared for a busy signal or a frozen computer screen.

Furthermore, a company's share price is likely to be influenced by traders who have little or no interest in the long-term viability of the company. In fact, they may not even own the stock. As mentioned above, speculators who think a stock is going to fall in price may profit by shorting the stock. They borrow shares from a brokerage firm's margin account, then sell them in the open market. If the speculator is correct and the stock price declines, they buy back the shares (called "covering the short") at a lower price and make a profit. Selling short is a specialty on Wall Street—but never a popular one. Sometimes speculators spread rumors about a company to push the stock price lower. Short sellers and short-term traders play all kinds of games in hopes of making a quick buck by manipulating stock prices.

Stock Prices Are Determined at the Margin

In my training as a professional economist, I have learned three vital principles that are highly applicable to the stock market: marginal analysis, expectations, and human action. Let's see how each of these concepts can be useful in analyzing the markets.

First, an often-overlooked reason stock prices can explode upward or plunge in a single day is this: *stock prices are determined at the margin.* What does this mean? The majority of investors may buy and hold for the long term, but it requires only a small number of buyers or sellers to move the price of a stock. Prices are quoted each minute on the exchange according to the number of buyers and sellers at any one time and what they are willing to bid. A sudden imbalance in the number of traders can move a stock rapidly one way or the other. Floor specialists on the New York Stock Exchange maintain an inventory of stock and commercial credit to cushion any liquidity crunch, but markets can still move very quickly with just a few traders, affecting the price of all shares.

For example, a total of 140 million shares of Yahoo were traded the day the share price fell 13 percent. That was five times its normal trading day volume of 22 million shares, but even then, 140 million shares represented only about 10 percent of all shares outstanding. Most Yahoo investors—90 percent of its stockholders—were happy to hold on to their investment. In short, a small percentage of shareholders sold Yahoo that day, and yet, because few investors were buying, the result was a major drop in the share price.

This principle of marginal behavior is well known to economists, but often ignored by the public and even company officials who own large blocks of stock. The marginality principle of pricing means that the market capitalization—the total number of shares multiplied by the share price—of a publicly traded company is unreal and unsustainable. It represents the bid and the offer prices of a *marginal* number of buyers and sellers during a normal day of trading. For example, suppose the president of a company, who owns 30 percent of the firm, suddenly decides to unload his position. Maybe he wants to diversify into other investments, such as real estate. Can the market bear this sudden increase in sales? Not likely. The price will probably start declining as he unloads his shares, and may even crash if he attempts to sell all his shares at once.

In a sense, the prices of all liquid assets are fanciful. The value of your brokerage account is not actually real until you sell your securities and convert them into cash.

Stock Prices Are Always Forward Looking

A second reason a company's stock may not reflect its current business condition is expectations. Because shareholders can sell part or all of their shares at any time, stock prices are much more sensitive to future expectations.

What determines stock prices? Many investors, following the advice of Ben Graham or other "fundamentalists," believe that prices are ultimately determined by the fundamentals of the company—sales, profit margins, market share, etc. . . . And in the long run, they are right. Value ultimately determines the weight of every publicly traded company. Finance professors and security analysts have proven beyond a doubt that earnings per share do determine the value of stocks over a five- or ten-year period.

But such figures may not be helpful in the short run. Why? Largely because company fundamentals—sales and earnings—reflect what has happened in the past and the present, but not the future. Yet, while we are judged by the past, we must live into the future. Granted, history often repeats itself, but never in quite the same way. The future is uncertain—and sometimes scary. The real question investors must always ask is: What is the outlook for a given stock over the next few months or years? For fundamentalists, this includes the all-important question: What is the outlook for sales and earnings over the next quarter or year? In a sense, then, investing in the stock market is nothing more than a bet on the future, which is full of surprises.

This is an important part of The Lesson. Here's an example: fundamentalists might argue that Yahoo stock fell 13 percent because investors thought that the company could not keep growing as fast as it did in the past. The next five years of earnings are more important than the last five years of earnings. So why did the mining company Miramar's shares advance 50 percent? Again, fundamentalists might have divined that investors expected Miramar to produce tons of gold at a substantial profit in the next few years, and commodity prices were moving up at the time. It's more about expectations than the most recent quarterly earnings report.

Stock market crashes often illustrate this principle of expectations. For example, the 1929 crash occurred at a time when the "new era" economy of the Roaring Twenties was booming. Contrary to popular belief, the crash by itself did not cause the Great Depression; rather it was a reflection of expectations that severe economic problems were awaiting in the near future. Not all crashes are that prescient, however; the October 1987 crash had little impact on the economy, and was simply the result of a temporary marginal sell off.

Human Action: Rational or Irrational?

The third principle of investing is human action. All activity in the stock market, including prices and volume, is determined by human decision-making. Those decisions can be incredibly complex and may even be irrational, such as buying at the top of a market out of a sense of euphoria or selling at the bottom in a panic. But this does not mean that stock prices are random, even in the short-term, as many analysts insist. All human action is purposeful, including the buying and selling of stocks, even though an outsider might not know the motive of the buyer or seller. Humans are neither machines nor simply animals, but have free will and the ability to adapt and change their minds. They can ignorantly lift stock prices up to crazy levels, or push them far below book value. They can learn from their mistakes and alter their outlook or behavior. As the Chinese philosopher Lin Yutang says in *The Importance of Living*, "The human mind is charming in its unreasonableness, its inveterate prejudices, and its waywardness and unpredictability."

Shareholders don't need a single, collective reason to buy or sell. They can add a stock to their portfolio or drop it for an endless variety of reasons—a rumor, a fad, a geopolitical event, a newsletter recommendation, an earnings reports, a line on a chart, or some "mad money" TV commentator. Or they may sell for personal reasons—to pay taxes, buy a house, pay for an emergency medical bill, or invest in another hot stock. This makes stock price fluctuations very difficult to predict—but they are not random. There is a reason behind every buy and sell decision, and the sum total of these decisions move stock prices one way or another.

But if a company is privately held, it has no shares to sell on an exchange, so the number of erratic reasons for selling are substantially less than for public firms. Thus, taking a company public can create mayhem in the financial markets, and stocks can trade for years at prices far removed from their fundamental or intrinsic value. Sometimes the owners of a public company get so fed up that they buy up the outstanding shares and go private again to avoid the strain of public trading and the scrutiny of Wall Street analysts.

Institutional investors also play a critical role in determining the market value of a company. Insurance companies, mutual funds, pensions, university endowments, and large money managers (including hedge funds) represent half the market in the United States. These pros can issue a buy or sell signal for 10 million shares at a time, far more than an individual investor can control. More and more institutions are using computer generated trades to make portfolio decisions, resulting in increased volatility. These kinds of institutional investors often engage in a herd mentality, following whatever is popular at the time.

Macroeconomic Events and Geopolitics

The following is a list of reasons, based on human action and perception, that stock prices are much more volatile than a company's fundamentals.

Macroeconomic events

Changes in economic policy, interest rates, and geopolitics can influence the markets across the board. As a financial economist, I take a top-down approach to investing. Along with geopolitics, macroeconomics is the most important overarching issue affecting investments. When it comes to deciding whether to buy a stock, mutual fund, or country fund, I first want to decide what the macro climate is like. Is it favorable for this company, fund, or industry? Sure, some stocks buck the trend, but as an investor, I want as much going for me as possible.

Economic reports are also vital. Securities firms, economists, and government agencies report on inflation, economic growth, foreign trade, leading indicators, consumer/business spending, job claims, employment figures, and so forth. GDP growth rates are reported quarterly. Good news can send stocks higher, and bad news can send them lower—although this is not always the case. Fiscal policy, such as tax rates on dividends and capital gains, Social Security reform, and other legislation likewise can affect stock prices.

Geopolitical events

Wars and terrorist threats, speeches by political leaders, natural disasters, national elections, international banking, economic crises, nationalization of corporate assets, the death of a prime minister—all these affairs can have a major impact on investor decisions. The 1907 panic was caused by President Teddy Roosevelt's threats to break up the Rockefeller trusts and other big businesses. The Dow fell almost 7 percent on December 7, 1941, when the Japanese attacked Pearl Harbor. In October 1957 stocks declined 10 percent after the Soviets launched the Sputnik rocket. The sudden fall of the Berlin Wall in late 1989 precipitated a sharp rise in the German stock market. A week after the September 11 terrorist attacks, when the New York Stock Exchange reopened, the Dow fell 7 percent. Instability in the Middle East frequently causes sharp rises in commodity prices and military defense stocks. Free-trade agreements with Mexico and Chile have encouraged rising markets in Latin America.

When investing internationally, look to countries that are favorable toward the industries that interest you. Stocks perform best in politically stable nations that limit the size and scope of government intervention and let entrepreneurs flourish. Highly regulated and highly taxed economies should be avoided.

The Federal Reserve

Central bank policies established by the U.S. Federal Reserve ("The Fed"), the Bank of England, the Bank of Japan, or the Central European Bank can also exert a major influence on market conditions and the global economy. Through their monetary policy and their control over short-term interest rates, the money supply, and currency values, central banks can significantly impact not only the stock and bond markets, but the real estate and commodity markets as well.

A "tight money" policy—that is, raising interest rates and reducing the amount of money in circulation—can send even highly profitable stocks lower. To the contrary, an "easy money" policy—lowering interest rates and printing more money—often lifts stocks. However, an excessive "easy money" policy can cause stock prices to drop in anticipation of higher inflation down the road. Fear of higher inflation can cause commodity prices and gold stocks to skyrocket and traditional stock and bond markets to plummet, as it did in the inflationary 1970s. Fed policy can even cause a depression, as it did in 1929–33, or it can keep a stock market crash from causing a depression, as it did in 1987 and 2000–01.

Historically, the stock market has been vulnerable to frequent changes in monetary policy made by the central bank. By switching repeatedly between "easy money" and "tight money," the Fed and other central banks can create a boom-bust cycle. Such changes, which can wreak havoc in the financial markets and the economy, should be monitored closely by investors.

I watch Fed policy very carefully in my newsletter, *Forecasts & Strategies*. You would be wise to follow the old saying on Wall Street, "Don't fight the Fed." For example, if the Fed lowers interest rates below the "natural rate of interest" (the interest rate for credit under a noninflationary environment), it creates conditions favorable toward an artificial boom or asset bubble in certain classes of investments, such as technology stocks, real estate, or commodities. Speculators often find big opportunities to profit under such conditions.

As Austrian economists Ludwig von Mises and Friedrich Hayek have shown, these speculative booms cannot last, and investors who stay too long in these sectors can get burned. The Asian currency crisis in 1997 was largely caused by easy credit mixed with local currencies tied to the U.S. dollar at a fixed rate. Similarly, the real estate boom of 2001–05 was fueled in part by the Fed's decision to create low short-term interest rates (as low as 1 percent). An economy built on easy money and excessive debt is structurally imbalanced and will inevitably slump. There is no free lunch, as economist Milton Friedman often said.

In the beginning of this book, I asked why it is that a strong employment report can send the market sharply lower, while slower GDP growth can cause a stock market rally. Now we see what causes this strange phenomenon. In a period of high inflation, a strong employment report may be viewed as inflationary and unsustainable, pointing to the possibility that the Fed will have to adopt a tighter money policy in the future. The stock market, anticipating the future, declines. On the other hand, a slowdown in GDP growth may suggest that inflation is not an immediate problem and that the Fed will ease its policy in the future, thus enticing more investment in the market.

Changes in Business Fundamentals

A company's or sector's fundamentals are another important cause of stock price movement. This is because most analysts and a large percentage of investors are educated in the fundamental value of stocks. They analyze quarterly reports on sales and profits, and watch for announcements of new products. Deals with suppliers and customers also tend to move stocks, sometimes dramatically. Investors also rely on brokers and investment advisors who have gathered the information and rendered their opinions based on fundamental analysis.

However, it is worth noting that quarterly earnings reports can be quite unpredictable. For example, it is not unusual for the Value Line Investment Survey to change a rating on a stock due to a "surprise" factor. But such surprises, naturally, may still be anticipated by individual investors and analysts who have inside information or have received some other indication of upcoming good news. And even the announcement of good news is not necessarily a guarantee of higher stock prices, as we noted in the beginning of this book, for many other considerations can offset any single positive development.

Other Reasons Why Stock Prices Can Skyrocket or Collapse, Irrespective of Market Fundamentals

Here are some other reasons why a stock's price may diverge—sometimes dramatically and surprisingly—from its fundamental enterprise value.

The list, you will see, is exceptionally long. Note that none of these reasons have anything to do with current earnings, sales, new products, or the debt of the company, although they may affect future financials.

Insider buying or selling

Remember those company officers who hold large positions in their own company? When their shares become tradable, they can sell their position at any time as long as they report the trade to the government. They may sell for any number of reasons unrelated to the company's prospects. Suppose the CEO is getting a divorce, or perhaps sees a better opportunity for his money. Or maybe he decides to retire and cash in his investment. Either way, if he sells a large enough block of stock, it will send the share price down sharply. On the other hand, an insider might expect better sales and earnings and start buying stock, causing the price to rise—especially if analysts tracking insider trades take notice.

Regular sales of stocks by insiders and company employees can put a drag on a good company for years. For example, Microsoft, one of the largest tech companies in the world, recently reported a profit margin of 31 percent and earnings growth of 16 percent. On the surface, the stock looks cheap for a tech company. Its price to earnings ratio—a common way of valuing a stock by dividing the share price by the company's earnings per share—is just 18. Yet the stock has floundered for five years. It never moves much one way or another. Investors keep holding on, thinking the stock will eventually break on the upside, but they wait in vain. The reason? Bill Gates, the president, keeps selling huge blocks of stock every couple of months to finance his charitable foundation. In one month, he sold 40 million shares worth $1 billion!

Official buy or sell recommendations

Major brokerage firms and regional security companies issue frequent buy and sell recommendations, and a new announcement of an upgrade or downgrade may move a stock, sometimes dramatically. Stock prices can be influenced by recommendations from popular stockbrokers, respected analysts and economists, newsletter writers, magazine columnists, and television or radio personalities. This group may include technical traders and chartists, and computerized sell or buy programs that are geared to sudden profit taking.

Rumors

Unconfirmed rumors spread by company officers, shareholders, traders, message boarders, and the government often move stock prices. If it is rumored that a president or prime minister is ill, stocks may suddenly drop, at least temporarily. If there is an unconfirmed story that the government is investigating the president of a major company, it could hurt the company's share price. A rumor that a certain company is a takeover target could cause the stock to rise. Tips are commonplace, and in the age of instant messaging and weblogs, they don't have to be substantiated to affect the markets.

Competition

A firm that is doing just fine may nevertheless see its stock price decline after a competitor announces an increase in market share, the introduction of a new product, or the winning of a major bid. The fear is that the company will lose future sales to competitors and its earnings will decline. When the Venetian hotel and casino chain won a license to establish a resort in Singapore, for example, its stock jumped 10 percent, while the stock prices of its competitors dropped.

New issues

Without warning, a company may announce plans for a new issue of stock to raise investment capital and expand business. Usually investors view new issues negatively in the short term, as they increase the number of shares and dilute the value of existing shares.

Fads

Certain sectors can be hot or out of favor. Some investment philosophies or strategies become fashionable on both Wall Street and Main Street, and they can last for years. During my thirty-five-year career in this business, such fads have included the "Nifty Fifty," the "Six Year Gold Cycle," the "Dogs of the Dow," "Diamonds (and Rare Coins) Have Never Had a Downtick," and the dotcom craze of the 1990s. During an investment craze, certain "in" stocks sell far beyond their intrinsic value, while out-of-favor but good companies languish in price. When the fad ends, the "in" stocks collapse, and the value plays recover. The danger lies in not knowing when the fad will end or what new one will take its place. The news media often plays a major role in this frenzy. Groupthink is commonplace, as shown in the classic work on the subject of fads and investing, *Extraordinary Popular Delusions and the Madness of Crowds*, by Charles Mackay.

Momentum trading

Many traders and speculators use computerized technical strategies unrelated to company or economic fundamentals to buy and sell stocks and stock indexes. Following the rule "buy strength, sell weakness," stock jockeys may adopt a "momentum" trading system to buy hot stocks and to dump shares that have seemingly lost their potential. Fast money often results in some stocks skyrocketing far above their value, or good stocks falling sharply. Mechanical program trading that triggers specific buy and sell points constitutes more than 30 percent of all trades at this time. With sharply lower costs of trading, commissions, and bid-ask spreads, it's easier than ever to buy and sell regardless of economic fundamentals.

Computer error is also a potential cause of price volatility. For example, in 2003 a computer program mistakenly entered thousands of trades in a Nasdaq stock, causing the stock to trade 3 million shares in a twelve minute period, and pushing the stock price down from $57 to

$39. It recovered at the end of the trading day after the mistake was discovered, but many investors were stopped out and sustained big losses in the meantime.

Leverage

Stocks are often purchased with borrowed money, called buying "on margin." Large hedge funds often leverage their position with derivatives and credit lines. After a stock falls steeply, say, by 15 percent, it may fall another 15 percent as speculators sell to cover their margin calls (demands from brokers for cash deposits to cover an investor's losses). A sudden sell off can even hurt good stocks, which sometimes need to be sold to cover margin calls.

Tax selling

Investors can save on taxes by selling stocks that have fallen in price to offset gains from stocks they have sold at a profit. Tax selling is often done near the end of the year, especially in December, and often pushes share prices way below their fundamental value. In January, they usually recover as tax selling ends and bargain hunters jump aboard.

Short sellers

Traders look for opportunities to profit by shorting overvalued stocks on the assumption that the price will soon decline. A small number of them employ a variety of underhanded tactics such as spreading negative rumors about the stock on the Internet, or otherwise manipulating stock prices down to where the stop orders—automatic orders to sell a stock if it falls to a certain price—will cause a rash of selling.

Merger/takeover target

When a merger/takeover is announced, the company being taken over usually advances in price because the buyout offer is higher than the current stock price. At the same time, the company doing the buying usually falls in price because of the cost involved. Occasionally, they both go up in price.

Departure or hiring of a CEO

If an active CEO or other high-ranking executive who is crucial to the performance of a firm dies or leaves, it can leave a leadership gap. Investors will often sell the stock in anticipation of the uncertainty associated with replacing him. When a new CEO is hired, the price of the stock will reflect investors' confidence, lack of confidence, or uncertainty in the leader. A stock will often advance significantly if investors perceive that a strong, new leader has come in to turn around a company.

Government investigations, lawsuits, and bad publicity

Scams, frauds, and misrepresentations can invite government investigations or lawsuits and thus damage a company's reputation and share price. If a judge imposes a major fine, or dismisses a serious case, the share price can make a major move in either direction. A front page story in the *Wall Street Journal* or *Forbes* could send a stock skyrocketing—or collapsing. Even more perversely, if a big event is anticipated, the market may act before the incident, and then move in the opposite direction when the event is finally announced. This is the source of the refrain, "Buy on the rumor, sell on the news."

Thus, a publicly traded firm may be engaged in business as usual, and yet the market valuation of the company may vary dramatically from day to day, depending on any or all of these factors. As Bernard Baruch once told a Congressional committee, "Whether stocks rise or fall is determined by innumerable forces and elements, by economic conditions, the actions of governments, the state of international affairs, the emotions of people, even the vagaries of the weather."

In conclusion, you can see myriad reasons why Wall Street is different from Main Street, why the business of investing is very distinct from investing in a business. Price often trumps value in the short run. Ben Graham summed it up best: "Most of the time common stocks are subject to irrational and excessive price fluctuations in both directions, as the consequence of the ingrained tendency of most people to speculate or gamble—i.e., to give way to hope, fear and greed." And this false hope, fear, and greed can destroy people's fortunes and lives.

Six

HAS WALL STREET BECOME ANOTHER LAS VEGAS?

> "The typical investor has usually gathered a good deal of half-truths, misconceptions, and just plain bunk about successful investing."
>
> PHILIP A. FISHER, *COMMON STOCKS AND UNCOMMON PROFITS*

When I teach investing at Rollins College or Columbia University, I begin my course by holding up two pieces of paper. In one hand I hold up a lottery ticket and in the other a stock certificate. I ask, "Are these two pieces of paper mostly the same, or are they mostly different?"

The students usually make good arguments on both sides.

Given the volatility and wide variety of risks involved in selecting stocks, some observers refer to the stock market as a glorified gambling hall. Several years ago, *Business Week* labeled the financial markets part of a "Casino Society." People bet on anything, without regard to fundamentals and real values. I have a book in my library entitled *Wall Street: The Other Las Vegas*, by stock market expert Nicolas Darvas, who calls the market "a gambling house peopled with dealers, croupiers and touts on one side, and with winners and suckers on the other."

Many of my fellow economists feel the same way. I talked with Milton Friedman, the famous monetarist and defender of the free market, soon after the October stock market crash in 1987. He, too, labeled the stock market a casino that had little to do with the real economy. "The stock market is grossly overvalued as it affects the economy," he told me. His remarks reminded me of the statement of another Noble Prize economist, Paul Samuelson, who said, "The stock market has predicted nine of the last five recessions."

If the stock market is essentially a gambling hall that serves no social or economic function other than the pleasure of rolling the dice, some social philosophers have suggested that it be abolished, or at least highly taxed and regulated. Marxists see no value in the stock market, which they regard as a bourgeois pleasure dome. The old Russian stock exchange in Leningrad was made into a museum by the Soviet authorities. Now that Leningrad has transformed back into St. Petersburg, the Russian stock market is thriving again.

We noted earlier that John Maynard Keynes, an avid speculator himself, regarded the stock market as a game of chance whose outcome is unpredictable and often irrationally acted upon by "animal spirits." Market uncertainty ostensibly leads to waves of excessive pessimism and optimism, potentially damaging business expectations in the real economy. Keynes and his followers recommended the introduction of a "substantial government transfer tax" on all stock transactions to discourage speculative fever. Other economists and even some Wall Street analysts recommend a higher tax on short-term stock profits to encourage more buy-and-hold investing. Many governments do in fact tax short-term capital gains at a higher rate than long-term gains.

Is the stock market really just a casino? It sometimes appears that way, but outward appearances can be deceiving. Peter Lynch, famed fund manager of the Magellan Fund and author of One Up on Wall Street, once observed, "Although it's easy to forget sometimes, a share of stock is not a lottery ticket. It's part ownership in a business." There are essential differences between gambling and the stock market, between Las Vegas and Wall Street, but as I have demonstrated in this book, the differences are sometimes elusive.

And therein lies both danger and opportunity. The financial markets can be used as a gambling vehicle, as they were in the early twentieth century with the bucket shops—betting sheets on stocks that operated purely as bets, with no stock ownership involved. Indeed, many technical trading systems are based on mathematical formulas similar to betting schemes. Moreover, the derivative markets (options and futures markets) have become so removed from companies' fundamentals that they have all the appearances of a gigantic gambling casino. The stock options market in particular has become a main focus of this gambling mentality.

Differences Between Wall Street and Las Vegas

Of course, even if some people do approach investing as a form of gambling, there are a number of crucial differences between the stock market and a game of craps or blackjack.

In gambling, for every winner there is a loser.

In most casino bets, if a player wins, then the house has to lose, and vice versa. That's not the case with investments. A company may increase in value due to intelligent business decisions, and the stock price may rise accordingly. An investor may hold a stock for a year and then sell it for a 30 percent profit to another investor, who may in turn hold it for a year and sell his shares for a 20 percent profit. This can go on indefinitely if the underlying company steadily rises in value, which some firms do. Admittedly, the first seller has "lost" the potential to gain another 20 percent. But he can put his money to use somewhere else, possibly earning even more.

In a casino, the odds are always against the player.

Casinos make money by offering games where the odds always favor the house. But an investor can substantially change the odds in his favor

through superior knowledge or technique. Jesse Livermore, the speculator, learned this: "My great discovery was that a man must study general conditions, to size them so as to be able to anticipate probabilities.
I was no longer betting blindly, but earning my successes by hard study
and clear thinking." Admittedly, gamblers can increase their chances of
winning through card-counting and other techniques. But such methods, if they are too successful, will get a player banned from the casino.
In investment markets, in contrast, a top performing speculator is not
limited by his success.

Investors can make money in the stock market over the long term.

Investors can reel in long-term profits. This is not usually the case at a
casino, where players tend to lose the longer they stay in a game. The
odds favor the house in a game of craps, blackjack, or roulette, so that
the longer you play, the greater your chances of losing. That's why good
gamblers walk away from the table once they achieve a significant
profit. Poker, however, is an exception to this rule: luck is involved, but
intelligent poker players can win more often than they lose in the long
run, and can improve their game through experience and skill.

Investors with adequately diversified portfolios have earned a positive
return on their money over the long term. This assumes that investments
are in a free-enterprise country that encourages ownership in stocks; the
threat of onerous regulation makes long-term strategies risky in con-
trolled economies. Of course, people who don't invest properly can easily lose money in the long run even in U.S.-based stocks. Concentrating
too much money in too few companies or buying expensive stocks with
high P/E ratios are common routes to long-term investing failure.

The stock market has traditionally been a good
leading indicator of nationwide economic performance.

The S&P 500 stock index is used as one of the leading economic indicators in the United States, and similar indexes are used in other coun-

tries. As an active participant in the economy's capital stock, the stock market is used to finance new technology, production processes, and construction. Playing the roulette wheel and other gambling action, on the other hand, is pure consumption. Thus, action in Las Vegas, a small sector of the entertainment industry, is not really a leading indicator of anything.

Stock market activity reflects national optimism or pessimism.

Nations whose economies are performing well are likely to experience a bull market in stocks and a strong currency. On the other hand, nations facing serious economic troubles are likely to suffer from a bear market and a falling currency. The vagaries of Las Vegas casinos, in contrast, reflect little of the national mood.

While a casino represents pure consumption, the stock market represents the capital market.

The capital market is crucial to a modern, developing nation. Remember that stocks are issued initially to raise capital for a company providing goods, services, and employment. Even the secondary market for stocks can benefit the company, especially if it offers stock or stock options to its employees. Invariably, countries without a stock market are underdeveloped and have low standards of living. If the stock market were abolished in major industrial nations, or discouraged through confiscatory taxation, it would likely provoke massive layoffs and a depression as the sources of capital dried up. Many new company expansion plans would come to a quick halt. Granted, companies could raise investment funds from the bond market or through bank loans, but the cheapest and most liquid form of capital—issuing stock to the public—would no longer exist.

In short, despite the appearance of a gambling mentality in the stock market, the securities market plays a crucial role in a nation's capital development and business expectations.

Nevertheless, it is interesting to note that many successful investors were gamblers in their youth—John Templeton, John Kluge, and Warren Buffett, for instance. As *Forbes* magazine reported in its 1990 survey of the 400 richest people in America, "successful business people often turn out to be avid gamblers. Whether the game is poker, bridge, blackjack, or the horses doesn't matter, what matters is the game itself. The essence of these games—the systematic weighing of risks against rewards against mathematical probabilities—is the essence of business itself."

With the growing popularity of televised and online poker games, with more people traveling to Las Vegas and other gambling Meccas every year, and with the rise of "mad money" shows on prime time cable networks, it should not be surprising to see a gambling mentality entering the financial markets. While this may lead to some short-term market distortions, however, in the long run stock prices eventually return to their fundamental values.

Seven

THE PLUNGERS
AND THE PEACOCKS

"I found out that nobody was immune from the danger of making sucker plays."

JESSE LIVERMORE

"Don't think, just look!"

JAMES DINES, EDITOR, *THE DINES LETTER*

There is a growing fear that Wall Street is being dominated by short-term speculators, day traders, and programmers who use computerized technical systems that cause the markets to move further away from the business fundamentals of publicly traded companies. The gamblers, day-traders, and computerized systems often ignore company fundamentals and focus entirely on the tape—the internal action of stocks, commodities, and other investment vehicles—to determine tops and bottoms of markets. The more the public becomes enamored with this gambling mentality, the more vulnerable they are to a fall.

Some investors swear by these charting and quantitative techniques. Granted, I've met a few technical traders with an uncanny ability to use their computer charts to make a fortune, but it's always difficult to follow their methods. Investment author Jack Schwager calls them "market wizards." In his book of the same title, he describes a trader who turned $30,000 into $80 million; a fund manager who achieved five years of triple-digit percentage returns; a former security analyst who realized an average monthly return of 25 percent (over 1,400 percent annualized) over a seven-year period, primarily trading stock index futures; and an electrical engineering graduate from MIT whose largely computerized approach to trading earned his accounts an astonishing 250,000 percent return over sixteen years. (However, if you read their interviews in Schwager's book, you quickly discover that it's virtually impossible to figure out just how they trade profitably.)

This is an amazing group of speculators, and they attract a large following of investors hungry to make big money in the marketplace. Go to any large investment conference these days, and you will see how faddish the technical charts are. Dozens of chartists have exhibits with giant TV screens and a large room filled with charts, all overflowing with eager investors with green in their eyes willing to pay hundreds of dollars for their newest software programs. It's standing room only. Investors love to imitate the success of the market wizards.

What exactly is technical analysis and charting, and why is it so appealing? Looking over the financial pages of the *Wall Street Journal* or *Barron's*, one gets the impression that investing is a game of numbers and charts. There are charts on the prices of stocks, bonds, gold, currencies, and interest rates. The stock columns list highs and lows, closing prices, dividends, P/E ratios, and daily volume. Behind the numbers and charts are thousands of transactions between individual traders, or "human activity." But some investors don't think of the market in terms of human action. They see the market as a mathematically predictable pattern of numbers, believing that if you can just figure out the numbers pattern, you can be rich beyond your wildest dreams, whether on Wall Street, in the Chicago trading pits, or behind your own computer.

These number crunchers are the technical traders, constantly searching for the ideal system that will consistently beat the market. Their background is often in the physical or biological sciences—engineers or mathematicians by training, who search for regular, mechanical, and repeatable patterns, like a scientific experiment. However, aside from an extremely few "market wizards," they never seem to discover a magic elixir with lasting power. There's always some element of uncertainty about the market patterns.

The Strange Ways of the Old-Timers

Technical analysis is quite distinct from fundamental analysis. Fundamental analysis, as we have seen, looks at earnings reports, management, new product developments, and market conditions to determine the value of a security. Pure technical analysis determines whether an investment is a good buy based solely on *internal market data*—prior prices, trading volume, and other statistics that might determine supply and demand for a stock. Technical traders rely on graphs and charts of past and current behavior to suggest where a market is headed, whether it be an individual security, commodity, currency, interest rate, or an entire market index. They look at trend lines, point-and-figure charts, bar charts, and technical trading systems known as "Japanese candlesticks," among other sophisticated devices, to make short-term investment decisions.

In the past, the early technicians were true believers who dogmatically denied the value of fundamental or economic analysis. The market absorbs economic news, quarterly reports, and other financial data so quickly, they said, that few, if any, could profit from such information. The original chartist, John Magee, was an eccentric who boarded up his office window in Springfield, Massachusetts, to avoid completely any news from the outside world other than the ticker tape. He did not even care to know the name of the company he was trading, just its symbol on the exchange. The trader need not know the company, what it produces, or how it was financed, he maintained. "When I come into this office," he said, "I leave the rest of the world outside and concentrate entirely on my charts." He was fanatical about ignoring economic, political, or corporate news. He only wanted to keep a clear mind to focus on the technician's most fundamental tool, his charts.

Joe Granville, a die-hard technician, emphasized that pure technical charting is not relevant to fundamentals or macroeconomics. He used to tell his audiences, "What do interest rates have to do with the stock market? Absolutely nothing! What does inflation have to do with the market? Absolutely nothing! What do dividends have to do with the stock market? Absolutely nothing!" Other technical traders warn investors not to use fundamental analysis because doing research, reading the financial news, and studying economic and political trends only confuses you. The charts supposedly reflect all the fundamentals, so "Don't think, just look!" as technician James Dines is famous for saying. That is, look at the charts, and don't think about what's happening in the world because it will only cause you to make the wrong investment decisions.

You can see from the above comments why Wall Street firms originally considered technical traders to be one step away from astrologers or circus palm readers. Gradually, however, technicians have gained respect on Wall Street, and every major securities firm today has one or more technical chartist on staff.

Technical traders have also become more complex and sophisticated, and I've noticed recently that more are taking some fundamental and economic factors into account in their stock selection process. Similarly, many fundamentalists look at the charts before making a final buy or sell decision. Even Ken Fisher, a *Forbes* columnist and son of financial author Philip Fisher, maintains an element of technical analysis in his approach.

But technical analysts still consider the charts more important than the fundamentals. Technicians regard "Mr. Market" as fickle and uncertain; prices can change on a dime based on rational or irrational factors. Stocks are subject to constant fluctuations that have little to do with the fundamentals of a company. Technical analysis recognizes stock prices, either for individual stocks or for the market as a whole, as wholly psychological, and therefore the smart analyst will develop ways to judge the fickle attitude of investors. Keynes's view of the market as a special kind of beauty contest is appropriate here. In Keynes's beauty contest, the judges do not try to figure out who is the most beautiful, but who the other judges will think is the most beautiful. "Americans are apt to be unduly interested in discovering what average opinion believes average opinion to be." Therefore, the technical patterns are the key factors to look at, they say.

The Dow Theory

A wide variety of technical systems are currently in use. They include the Dow Theory, invented by Charles H. Dow, the original publisher of the *Wall Street Journal*, and William P. Hamilton, editor of the *Journal* in the 1920s. The Dow theory is based on Dow's fascination with the motions of the sea. He argued that the markets, like the ocean, can be divided into three major categories: tides, waves, and ripples. The tide represents the primary trend in the stock market; the waves represent the intermediate trend; and the ripples represent the day-to-day movements in stock prices. The most important task is to determine the primary trend. Here Dow theorists look for a market index, such as the Dow 30 Industrials, to be above its long-term average, and then for the Industrials index to be confirmed by the Transportation index (or vice versa). This technical model is followed and interpreted by many traders today.

Technical analysts also rely on many other indicators, such as moving averages and trend lines; head, shoulders and neckline formations; support and resistance levels; advance-decline ratios; cycle and wave analysis, including the Elliott Wave principle (named after R. N. Elliott); and bar charts and "Japanese candlesticks."

Support and resistance levels and volume statistics linked to price movements are major factors in technical analysis. For example, computerized sell programs can push a stock down as much as 20 percent in short order until buyers enter the market and give it "support." Stocks across the board are buoyed or hammered by these computerized trading systems, depending on technical patterns only.

Can the Charts Tell All?

Although the mechanical patterns in charting can make it appealing to investors who want an easy formula for making buy and sell decisions, I remain skeptical about the value of technical analysis. Chart patterns are sometimes so complex that even the technicians argue over what they mean. This has led to the common statement among technicians, especially after they have made a bad prediction, that "There is nothing wrong with the charts, only the chartists." I frequently remind technical traders that humans are not machines, and their free will always lends a certain degree of unpredictability to the future. Moreover, sudden catastrophic events, such as an earthquake, terrorist attack, or political assassination, will cause the markets to gyrate beyond the predictive power of any technical analyst.

Humans can learn from their past mistakes, and therefore past trends are no guarantee of future performance. Sure, humans repeat history (the kernel of truth in technical patterns), but never in the same way. Many academic studies of past price and volume trends demonstrate no justification for predicting future patterns. Behind every price formation of stocks and commodities is human action—individuals buying and selling. To the extent that chart patterns reflect market psychology, they may be useful, but this is not an exact science and never will be one.

Remember, you can't drive a car successfully by looking through the rear view mirror—unless of course the road is straight.

Over the years, I've encountered many technical traders who have forecast this or that, and a few have good track records. One of my favorite stories occurred in November 1987, a month after the stock market crash. I attended the annual New Orleans Investment Conference, sponsored by Jim Blanchard. At the conference, a famous technical guru came up to me with a copy of a chart taken from the *Wall Street Journal*. The chart was the daily price action of the Dow Jones Industrial Average. The analyst had carefully drawn lines on the chart to prove that the Dow Industrials was forming a massive "triangle." He spoke with great energy. "Look," he said, "once this triangle is complete, the Dow will either drop down or rise out of the triangle." He predicted that if the price rose out of the triangle, it meant that the Dow Industrials was headed for a new high. But if it dropped down below it, it would indicate that the Dow was headed for 1,200 or below. He said he had a feeling that it would drop down (he was a perennial bear), but he was willing to let the charts tell him.

Sure enough, a few days after the conference the Dow dropped below the triangle, indicating the beginning of another sharp drop in the market. But then something strange happened. The bear market he predicted never materialized. The Dow started rallying and never looked back, contrary to his "surefire" chart that had predicted disaster.

Here's another example of the pitfalls of pure technical analysis. In the late 1980s, Professor Ravi Batra came out with a bestseller, *The Depression of 1990*. He warned that the capitalist system goes through a regular cycle of boom and bust that lasts approximately sixty years, known elsewhere as the Kondratieff Cycle (named after a Russian economist). Since the last depression had begun in 1930, the next one could be pinpointed with precision—1990. The October 1987 crash confirmed Batra's worst fears. More was on the way. By 1990, the United States was in the beginning of a recession, and Batra's book gained notoriety. But a great depression à la 1930 never arrived, and Batra was discredited. By the mid-1990s, the market was riding high.

There is no mechanical reason why human beings are forced to go through a sixty-year cycle. The Kondratieff Cycle has proved to be elusive. Cycles in markets do exist, but there are fundamental reasons for them, and it's impossible to pinpoint how long they will last with any precision. Much depends on the actions of government officials. Each time is different. I recall commentators calling for a six-year gold cycle, or a ten-year real estate cycle. They are all ephemeral.

In sum, I believe technical charting and cycle analysis provide a hit-or-miss approach to Wall Street. Chartists can enjoy a fantastic record for a while, then suddenly fall apart, particularly if too many people become enamored with their technical approach, throwing the mechanics off balance.

A Tale of Two Crashes

Two financial events help us examine each investment philosophy and its impact: the 1987 crash and the 2000–03 tech crash. Let's examine each example in-depth and see what we can learn.

In the case of the October 1987 crash, the economic fundamentals were largely sound. Business across the nation was doing well, both before and after the meltdown. The economy was growing, inflation was under control, and interest rates were relatively stable. So why did the Dow Jones Industrial Average collapse by 22 percent on October 19, 1987? When the market opened the next day, there were literally no bids on IBM and other blue-chip stocks. Historians point to several factors, such as comments by the Treasury Secretary about a weak dollar and trade deficit, but I believe the crash can be blamed in large measure on an impulsive "Mr. Market" and the technical traders who encouraged mindless trading based on a line on a chart rather than business fundamentals.

In the summer of 1987, telephone-switching between no-load mutual funds was all the rage, based solely on a technical charting system of a 200-day moving average. Mutual fund investing was extremely popular, to the point where you couldn't go through a meal at home in the evening without a broker calling and telling you about the latest mutual fund. Few investors knew or cared about the companies the fund managers were buying. They just followed the line on a chart showing the mutual funds were moving higher. The brokerage business had become so successful that a book was released that year written by a Merrill Lynch broker entitled *No Experience Necessary: Make $100,000 a Year as a Stockbroker.* How? By buying and selling mutual funds.

As a result, the market got way ahead of itself, with everyone following the same charts. Then, when the price of mutual funds fell below their 200-day moving averaging on the Friday before the Monday crash, everyone sold at once. The October 1987 crash was purely a technician's folly, and with the business fundamentals sound, the market recovered within a few weeks.

The story is slightly different for the high tech bubble-bust in the late 1990s and early 2000s. The technical traders were in full stride as they pushed technology and Internet stocks sky-high into the year 2000, far above their fundamental values. In 2000, I remember being in the offices of Professor Burt Malkiel, author of *A Random Walk Down Wall Street,* as he showed me a chart of the price-earnings ratio of the Standard & Poors 500 Stock Index. It had gone through the roof, far above any previous level in history, including 1929. We looked at each other, and knew it couldn't last. Sure enough, within a few months stocks started falling, and within sixteen months, the heavily tech laden Nasdaq Index had fallen 70 percent.

Here the fundamentals came into play in a much stronger way, however, than they had in 1987. Many of the Internet and computer darlings of the 1990s saw their revenues and earnings decline sharply during this time of severe recession, which drove the prices of these Nasdaq stocks far lower than they would otherwise have gone. Once tech stocks started falling, the technical traders quickly headed for the exits, which probably pushed stock prices lower than they should have gone. It is the nature of chartists to be bullish one day and bearish the next, and that can be a source of instability.

In sum, technical traders played a large roll in the crash of 1987 and in the collapse of tech stocks in 2000–02. As skeptical as I am about these systems, I realize that technical trading, charting, and computerized programming are a growing "noise" in the marketplace that cannot be ignored. They can explain a lot about the short-term movements in stocks, and why stocks often sell far above their fundamental value.

In the next chapter, I discuss another reason why Wall Street and Main Street move in different directions; in this case, why investors have a tendency to overpay for "new economy" growth companies. It's called "The Growth Trap."

Eight

THE GROWTH TRAP

"Obvious prospects for physical growth in a business do not translate into obvious profits for investors."

BENJAMIN GRAHAM

"A cynic knows the price of everything, and the value of nothing."

OSCAR WILDE

In 2005, Jeremy Siegel, a professor of finance at the Wharton School and author of the bestseller *Stocks for the Long Run*, came out with a second book entitled *The Future for Investors*. In this new work, he came to a shocking conclusion: "New technologies, expanding industries, and fast-growing countries that stockholders relentlessly seek in the market often lead to poor returns." In other words, good companies do not necessarily translate into good investments. This chapter elaborates on this surprising, counterintuitive idea.

In recent years, Professor Siegel has been involved in empirical studies that constitute the new science of "behavioral economics." Several major financial economists are involved in this new, fruitful area of research, including Robert Shiller at Yale University, Richard Thaler at the University of Chicago, and Gary Smith of Pomona College.

Essentially, these experts reject the notion that individuals always act rationally in their own best interests. In reality, people often make mistakes, such as consuming too much, saving too little, getting too far into debt, failing to budget, failing to do sound financial planning, or even failing to make a will. In the investment world, they tend to pay too much, buy at the top, and sell at the bottom. Consequently, the stock market is not always efficient, and the public can overvalue or under-value certain investments. They often overpay for the newest and hottest stocks, while neglecting older, traditionally sound investments like oil stocks, consumer staples, and utilities. Let's look at several stud-ies that confirm this phenomenon.

Adding To and Subtracting From the Dow

Since 1928, Dow Jones has published the Dow Jones Industrial Aver-age, consisting of the top thirty blue-chip U.S. companies. Dow Jones, the proprietor of the DJIA, changes the average's composition every couple of years, depending on new trends and the profitability of indi-vidual firms. Until the 1980s, the DJIA companies were largely indus-trial, such as Exxon, General Electric, and Coca Cola. But since then, the mix has changed with the addition of several financial companies like Citigroup and AIG, entertainment giants like Walt Disney, and technology companies like Microsoft and Intel.

Over the past seventy-eight years, Dow Jones has made fifty substitu-tions in the Dow, with some odd and amazing results. For example, in 1932, at the bottom of the Great Depression, International Business Machines (IBM) was added. The company was suddenly removed in 1939, when it was doing poorly, only to return forty years later in 1979 after its fortunes had improved. Similarly, Coca Cola was added in 1932, removed in 1935, and returned in 1987. If IBM and Coke had remained in the Dow throughout, instead of being returned to the list at higher prices, the DJIA would be twice the size it is today. In a way, the DJIA, in an effort to hold only the best blue-chip stocks, has acted like the average investor—selling off its perceived losers and adding expected winners.

To emphasize this point, finance professor Gary Smith at Pomona College and his colleagues compared the return of two portfolios: a portfolio including all the stocks added to the Dow over the years, and another portfolio consisting of all the deleted stocks. They looked at the return of each portfolio after 250 trading days. Smith and his colleagues discovered that the deleted stocks earned an annualized return of 15.8 percent, compared to only 11.4 percent for the added stocks!

The Importance of "Regression to the Mean"

Professor Smith states, "Dow Jones tends to replace companies that are not in as dire straits as their recent performance suggests with companies that are not as stellar as they appear." Smith calls it "regression to the mean," a technical term used in probability and statistics. It means that when things are left to themselves, they tend to return to normal. In other words, they even out in the long run. For example, if you flip a coin and heads comes up five times in a row, you are not likely to roll five heads in a row the next time. Over time, your chances are going to "regress to the mean" of 50 percent heads, 50 percent tails.

In the financial markets, investors and institutions make a common error: they are too optimistic about good companies and too pessimistic about bad ones. Eventually this extreme situation rights itself. Shareholders (and many analysts) tend to dump poor companies after the firms have already reported their misdeeds, and their stock is likely to recover thereafter; likewise, investors tend to become overeager about companies that have already done extremely well, when the firms are likely to reach diminishing returns. They pay too much for the good companies, and as a result their returns are lackluster.

For example, Dow Jones added IBM in June 1979, after it had already made a huge run-up, and dumped Chrysler after it was threatened with bankruptcy. But IBM floundered in the 1980s, while Chrysler flourished after the government bailed it out. Another big blunder for the Dow occurred on November 1, 1999, when it added Microsoft, Intel, Home Depot, and SBC Communications to the list just as these stocks were approaching their all-time highs. Each moved sharply lower over the next seven years, and the DJIA went flat.

The Dangers of Investing in "Market Cap" Indexes

Investing in an index of hundreds of stocks, such as the Standard & Poors 500 Index, is a popular way to maximize returns. But investors can over-pay in index investing, too. The S&P 500 is a typical "market weighted" index (also known as a "market capitalization" or "market cap" index)—that is, the index price is determined by the market capitalization of each company in the index. This is a good idea during a bull market, but can result in poor returns during a bear market.

The problem is that market cap indexes tend to become overweighted in overvalued stocks and underweighted in undervalued stocks. Compare, for example, General Motors with Google. At the time of this writing, GM is by far the bigger company (number 3 in the Fortune 500), its sales are 32 times greater, and it has 57 times more employees than does Google, which isn't even in the top 200 companies in the United States. Yet Google is weighted much more heavily than GM in the S&P 500 because of its huge market capitalization. In fact, for every new dollar you invest in the S&P 500 Index, 7.5 cents goes into Google stock while only one cent goes into GM!

Cap-weighted stocks are never rebalanced in an index fund. This is fine in a bull market, where you're riding with your winners. But when the market turns down, as it inevitably does, market-cap index funds can drag down your performance. In the major bull market from 1995 to 1999, the Vanguard 500 Index Fund was ranked in the top 20 percent of all growth-income funds. In sharp contrast, during the bear market from 2001 to 2005, the same fund was ranked in the fourth quintile among growth-income funds!

Once again, these studies confirm the primary lesson of investing— Wall Street and Main Street often lead in separate directions.

"The Growth Trap"

Now let's look at a study by Jeremy Siegel called "The Growth Trap." Professor Siegel and his staff recently dissected the entire history of the S&P 500 Index since its inception in 1957. He wanted to test the established theory that the addition of new, vibrant companies to replace older, slower performing companies is the secret to the S&P 500 Index's strong long-term track record.

Like the Dow Jones Industrial Average, the S&P 500 Index is constantly updated. On average, twenty stocks a year are replaced with new ones, based on Standard and Poor's criteria for market value, earnings, and liquidity. By definition, the companies added are performing substantially better than the ones being removed. It's all part of the "creative destruction" process of capitalism. Interestingly, in 2000, at the peak of the technology bubble, forty-nine new firms were added to the index; in 2003, near the bottom of the bear market, the S&P 500 added only eight new firms. These annual changes transformed the composition of the index from largely industrial stocks to mostly financial and technology companies.

Siegel's project was a mammoth undertaking that required tracing the complex corporate histories of hundreds of successive firms that were acquired or distributed over several decades. He then compared the performance of two portfolios over nearly a fifty-year period: the "Survivors" portfolio, consisting of the original S&P 500 stocks, and the "Total Descendants" portfolio, comprised of companies that have been added over the years. He came to a startling conclusion, reported in his book, *The Future for Investors*: "The returns on the original firms in the S&P 500 beat the returns on the standard, continually updated S&P 500 Index and did so with lower risk.... The shares of the original S&P 500 firms have, on average, outperformed the nearly 1,000 new firms that have been added to the index over the subsequent half century."

How is this possible? According to Siegel, the reason is clear: Standard & Poors waited too long before adding these new growth companies to the index. Investors had bid up the price of these bold, new companies to an excessively high level, and by the time they were added to the S&P 500, investors were paying too much.

Admittedly, Standard & Poors was correct in noting that the new candidates for the index had better earnings, sales, and market values than the older firms. But they fell into the "growth trap" of adding too late the bold and the new to their index.

By the same token, the companies that had to be cut from the list had fallen so far down in price that when they were finally eliminated from the index, these "losers," unless they went out of business entirely, tended to recover and return to their true value. This is another example of "regression to the mean."

Peter Lynch warned that the "growth trap" is fairly universal. Individuals and institutions alike suffer from it. In his book, *One Up on Wall Street*, he noted that institutions wait to "buy Wal-Mart [until] there's an outlet in every large population center in America, fifty analysts following the company, and the chairman of Wal-Mart is featured in *People* magazine as an eccentric billionaire who drives a pickup truck to work. By then the stock sells for $40." Lynch was buying Wal-Mart when it was $4. He pointed out that most institutional buyers are restricted from buying small growth companies because the market capitalization is below their minimum. But once the price of the stock doubles or triples, the market capitalization is sufficiently high to qualify for purchase.

"This results in a strange phenomenon: large funds are allowed to buy shares in small companies only when the shares are no bargain."

IBM ("Big Blue") vs. Exxon ("Big Oil")

As an example of the "growth trap," Professor Siegel compares the total return over a fifty-three year period (1950-2003) of the technology giant IBM (known as "Big Blue") to Standard Oil of New Jersey (now Exxon/Mobil, known as "Big Oil"). He calls it a classic case of the "new" versus the "old." By every growth matrix used by security analysts, IBM beat out Standard Oil in terms of earnings, sales, cash flow, book value, etc. . . . Big Blue's earnings per year—the key indicator of long-term growth—rose more than three percentage points per year above that of Big Oil over the fifty-three years. During this time, the technology sector overall also grew much faster than the energy complex.

The results were shocking. While IBM beat out Standard Oil in terms of company statistics, Standard Oil returned a better performance for investors. One thousand dollars invested in IBM would be worth $961,000 at the end of this fifty-three-year period, while $1,000 invested in Standard Oil (Exxon) would have reached $1,260,000— 31 percent more. The returns assume reinvestment of all dividends, a key factor.

Why did this happen? Because investors consistently paid too much for IBM stock and underpaid for Standard Oil. They made the fundamental mistake of pushing the IBM stock price up excessively in relation to true value, while neglecting Standard Oil's relatively low price to value.

It all goes back to price-earnings ratios, a key to sound investing. As previously mentioned, P/E is defined as the price of a stock divided by the earnings per share. Investors tend to bid up the price of fast growing "new economy" stocks, so that growth stocks have high P/E ratios.

Siegel's study demonstrates a behavioral weakness: investors consistently make the mistake of chasing the high P/E stocks and avoiding the low ones. Inevitably, regression to the mean occurs: high P/E stocks like IBM eventually come back down to earth, despite their high earnings, while low P/E stocks like Standard Oil climb back up to their true worth. This is why *Forbes* columnist and investment manager David Dreman contends that the best contrarian approach to making money is to buy companies with low price-earnings ratios, in the 5-to-8 range.

Beware of Tech Stocks

In many ways, the "growth trap" is a paradox. The "new economy" stocks are the source of economic growth in the global economy, yet they continually disappoint investors. For each of the few high profile winners, there are hundreds of losers. And even the winners are usually overpriced. "Our fixation on growth is a snare," warns Professor Siegel. "The most innovative companies are rarely the best place for investors," because they constantly overpay for the privilege of owning shares in the bold and the new. Siegel warns in particular against buying any stocks with P/E ratios exceeding 100. Meanwhile, investors typically neglect the tried and true that are selling at low multiples and offer bargain opportunities.

Jeremy Siegel's work indicates that few technology or telecommunications stocks could be found in any list of the top twenty performers over a given ten-year period. In his bestseller *Beating the Street*, Peter Lynch wrote, "Finally, I note with no particular surprise that my most consistent losers were the technology stocks."

In short, investors don't live up to the old saying, "Buy low, sell high." When it comes to tech stocks, commodities, emerging markets, or any other hot investment area, they "buy high and hope to sell higher." More often than not, it is a formula that doesn't work; eventually investors are disappointed.

Is There a Workable Strategy for Investors Who Understand the Lesson?

So far, I've painted a complex, if not bleak, picture of the "Wall Street Jungle," as investment observer Richard Ney calls it. Fortunately, however, financial forces are at work that eventually bring stock prices in line with their fundamental business value. This tendency points to an overall method of investing—contrarian investing—that forms the basis of my main investing strategy, which I will introduce in Chapter 10. In the next chapter, we will break down the concept of contrarian investing, using historical examples to show how big profits can be made by acting against the conventional wisdom on the market.

Nine

THE CONTRARIANS

"It is contrary to one's natural reactions to be contrary to general opinions."

HUMPHREY B. NEILL, *THE ART OF CONTRARY THINKING*

Thus far, we have drawn several conclusions about the world of investing. Let's review:

1. A company's stock is far more volatile and risky than the underlying firm because every business owner and shareholder is capable of selling all or part of his shares at any time in the continuous auction we call the stock market.

2. Many variables influence a share price, often in a perverse way. Company fundamentals (including changes in technology) determine the long-term value of a stock, but in the short run, which can vary from a day to several years, stock prices can jump all over the place depending on fads, insider knowledge, economic and political events, trading systems, and recommendations by respected analysts and economists.

3. The stock market is increasingly being used as a casino or gambling house, encouraged by mindless technical charting games, day trading, and computerized programming schemes that are gaining in popularity. In a laissez-faire environment, where investors from around the world can move money from one place

to another, or from one investment to another, the stock market could become an increasingly dangerous place to invest your life savings. Although "buy and hold" strategies remain relatively safe since stocks tend to return to their fundamental business value, day trading and programmed trading make the markets much more volatile. Consequently, it becomes more difficult to "time" the market—there is a greater chance that investors will buy a stock near its peak and then sell out at a loss.

4. Beware of government policy. Changes in macroeconomic statistics can significantly affect your portfolio, no matter how successful a company is, and today more than ever monetary policy by central bankers can help or hurt your position. Furthermore, the Fed's policy toward interest rates and the money supply can create a treacherous boom-bust cycle that can whipsaw your investments and test your discipline.

What can an investor do to profit from these characteristics of Wall Street? One strategy that is often suggested is to be a "contrarian," or a "bargain hunter." The strategy of bargain hunting—buying cheap, undervalued stocks and avoiding more popular expensive ones—is an old one that's been advocated by many intelligent investors and behavioral economists, including J. Paul Getty, Bernard Baruch, John Templeton, Peter Lynch, Michael Price, David Dreman, and Eddie Lambert. Even "the Father of Value Investing," Ben Graham, who was not normally a bargain hunter, touted the advantages of being a contrarian. Contrarian investing is a popular strategy for identifying tops and bottoms of markets, and for profiting from the distortions caused by technical trading systems. But as with any strategy, there are no guarantees, and frankly, it isn't that easy.

You hear much these days about using contrarian indicators to make buy-and-sell decisions in the stock and commodity markets. Do these indicators work?

Many observers have noted the "madness of crowds," as Professor Charles Mackay put it in his classic work, *Extraordinary Popular Delusions and the Madness of Crowds*, first published in 1841 (and still in print). As examples of crowd psychology gone awry, contrarians frequently refer to Mackay's accounts of Tulip mania (1634-37), where a common tulip bulb in the Netherlands sold for more than six times the average Dutchman's annual wages; the South Sea Bubble (1711-17), where speculators drove up the price of shares in a British venture in South America to dizzying levels; and the Mississippi Bubble (1719-20), which entailed similar fantastic speculation in the shares of the Mississippi Company, a joint stock company in France established to trade with American lands.

The most recent example is the Internet/software bubble of the late 1990s, when the public pumped money in record volumes into tech stocks and funds. Dow Jones and Standard and Poors even added tech stocks to their indexes before tech stock prices crashed in the early 2000s. Similarly, the public withdrew heavily from Asian stocks in 2003, right near the bottom. The point is, people often act like lemmings, both in bull and bear markets. Following what the rest of the investors are doing will often lead you, along with them, right off a cliff.

The Father of Contrary Investing

One of my favorite books on this subject is *The Art of Contrary Thinking*, by Humphrey B. Neill, considered the "father of contrarian investing." Written in 1954, it is a delightful, philosophical book. Neill was an investment advisor who lived all his life in Vermont. A libertarian, he was a strong believer in laissez-faire government. Here are some excerpts from his book:

- What it comes down to in the final analysis is that a "crowd" thinks with its heart (that is, is influenced by emotions) while the individual thinks with his brain.

- It may appear to some readers as though the theory of contrary opinion, or the art of contrary thinking, is a cynical one. I do not think it is at all. I believe it is merely a matter of getting into the habit of looking on both sides of all questions and then determining from your two-sided thinking which is the more likely to be the correct version—which in turns leads to the correct conclusion.

- Is the public wrong all the time? The answer is decidedly, "No." The public is perhaps right more of the time than not. In stock market parlance, the public is right *during* the trends but wrong at both ends!

- It is probably safe to say, however, that it is wiser to be early than to be late…a contrary opinion is usually ahead of time.

- If one relies on the Theory of Contrary Opinion for accurate *timing* of his decisions, he frequently will be disappointed…. There is no known method of timing economic trends.

- If the habit of contrary thinking does no more than to teach us to develop our own resources—and to like to be alone occasionally—it would be worthwhile…. The vast majority of people dislike to be alone.

- Nothing, perhaps, is more frustrating to an individualist than to be mired in a modern group-led, massive, corporate organization…. Nonconformists are in the tiny minority.

Joe Kennedy as a Lone Wolf

One of the extraordinary characters of high finance was Joe Kennedy. A strict contrarian, he was perhaps the most successful speculator during the 1929-32 stock market debacle. Kennedy seemed to have an ideal temperament for speculating—"a passion for facts, a complete lack of sentiment, a marvelous sense of timing," as a confidante once said.

According to various accounts, Kennedy stayed in the market until late 1928, when he sold most of his RKO "A" shares and options, netting several million dollars. He spent the winter of 1928–29 at his second home in Palm Beach, Florida, an estate he had purchased at a bargain price after the Florida real estate crash. Kennedy decided not to reinvest as the market rose in 1929, but rather to stay in cash. "Only a fool holds out for top dollar," he once said. In the summer of 1929, his decision to stay out was reaffirmed when he saw that everyone, even the shoeshine boys, was talking about hot stocks. "Then and there, so ran his recollection, he decided that a market anyone could play, and a shoeshine boy could predict, was no market for him," wrote biographer Richard Whalen.

Kennedy reportedly sold short during the long market descent in the early 1930s and made another million dollars. He re-entered Wall Street on the long side in early 1933, six months after the market had bottomed. Talk about good timing. How did he do it? By contrary investing.

Four Stages of Investment Psychology

Thus far, I've written a lot about investor psychology because it is a key element of the business of investing. Because investors have the ability and liquidity to sell all or part of their shares at any time, the intelligent investor must understand the temperament of the investing public.

Crowd psychology can be divided into four stages:

1. Fear
2. Caution
3. Confidence
4. Euphoria

Fear and euphoria represent the two rare extremes, while caution and confidence are the moderate states that usually characterize the market.

Stock market and commodity crashes are examples of the fear phase, when emotionally charged investors panic and throw caution to the wind, selling out at any price. It's usually a poor judgment. In the early 1980s, for example, the investing public was in a very negative mood. Price inflation was in the double digits, and the U.S. economy was struggling with interest rates reaching as high as 21 percent. President Reagan's tax cuts didn't seem to be working; the deficit was growing at an alarming rate. The Dow Jones Industrial Average was around 700, and numerous pundits predicted it would collapse to 300 or lower. Many investors gave up and sold out. Then, in the summer of 1982, as most investors were fleeing the traditional stock and bond markets, the market turned around and never looked back. It soared to new heights during the Reagan years, except for the brief crash on October 19, 1987.

By contrast, while the general public feared the stock and bond markets in the early 1980s, it was in love with gold. As gold approached $800 an ounce, investors became euphoric about precious metals. In the 1970s, with the price of gold freed from the international gold standard and with inflation rising to double digit rates, gold bugs had been confident in predicting a bull market in gold and silver. This period was followed by a euphoric rise in the price of gold, reaching $850 an ounce in January 1980, while silver climbed to $50 an ounce. At this point, the general public was begging to buy gold and silver; I remember many casual acquaintances approaching me in social settings and asking how to buy gold. But this turned out to be the top of the market, and precious metals dropped sharply soon afterward.

These euphoric episodes are not uncommon on Wall Street. As previously discussed, the soaring prices of Nasdaq-listed tech stocks throughout the 1990s was another example of a herd mentality on Wall Street ultimately ending in despair for many investors.

Remember Humphrey Neill's refrain, "The public is right during the trends, but wrong at both ends."

Searching for Extremes

The contrarian investor tries to buy at the extreme "fear" stage and sell at the extreme "euphoria" stage. In between, an upward or downward trend is in place, and the public is right most of the time. One of the most difficult judgments to make in this business is recognizing when the extremes occur. As the old Wall Street saying goes, "They don't ring a bell at the top of a market."

Identifying the top or bottom of a market is more art than science, and it requires experience. To determine a primary bottom—the end of a long bear market—seasoned investors look for panicky news, bearish readings in investment polls, heavy insider buying, and large mutual fund reserves. A crash is usually a short-term bottom and a good time to buy. Similarly, to anticipate a market top, speculators look for the opposite: euphoric news, bullish readings in investment polls, heavy insider selling, and low cash reserves by mutual funds.

But being a contrarian is not easy. Timing the market tops and bottoms is complicated, since trends can last for years and excessive highs in stock prices can become even more extreme before falling to a more reasonable level.

Sensing the top of a market is very tricky. Just because stocks are at an all-time high does not mean that the top has been reached. For example, Arnold Bernard pointed out in 1959 in his book, *The Evaluation of Common* Stocks, that at that time the Dow Jones Industrial Average was selling at its highest point in history. The average stock was selling at twenty times earnings and yielded only 3.2 percent. He noted that these indicators were identical to those in 1929, just before the crash. Bernard concluded that stocks in 1959 were "radically overvalued." His analysis turned out to be excessively bearish. Stocks went on to reach much higher levels, and no 1929-style crash occurred. Bernard was a seasoned investment advisor and founder of the respected Value Line Investment Survey, but even he had misread the markets and the psychology of the investing public.

One of the biggest difficulties in searching for bargains and under-valued stocks is recognizing the difference between what is *temporarily* undervalued and what is *permanently* undervalued. Some investments take years to recover, or never bounce back at all. I recall an unortho-dox investment guru recommending real estate in Rhodesia (now Zim-babwe) in the late 1970s, based on Baron Rothschild's dictum, "Buy when blood is running in the streets." He figured that prices were so low there during the bloody revolution that real estate was a steal. He talked about an estate with a mansion, gardens, fruit trees, and servants for only $50,000. What happened? The real estate market there didn't recover for decades, and in the meantime the political climate made it dangerous even to visit the estate.

Can Everyone Be a Contrarian?

Why can't everyone be a contrarian? By the market's very nature, only a small minority of investors can be successful contrarians. Everyone cannot get out at the top because all prices are based on *marginal* buy-ing and selling, as noted in Chapter Five. If everyone tries to get out at the top, prices will immediately collapse. The only way accurate infor-mation about a future financial event can be helpful to the speculator is if, in the words of Ludwig von Mises, "he alone has it while all other people are still bullish."

In the stock market, since potentially everyone can sell at any time, a successful contrarian must be one of the few to recognize the top and sell at that moment. Conversely, because everyone can potentially buy, one must be one of the few to realize a stock has bottomed out and sell before everyone else does the same. Thus, only a minority of investors can get out at the top or buy at the bottom, and they must do so before all the other investors discover the overvalued or undervalued situation.

Let's extend this reasoning a little further. Only a small minority can be successful contrarians and beat the market. The majority can never beat the market consistently, because the market is, by definition, everyone. In the financial markets, you are always competing against other investors. There's a perpetual race to be the number one contrarian. Although everyone can make money when the market goes up, only a relative few can beat the market.

A Workable Solution!

The key to success is to search constantly for better information than the next investor and for a correct understanding of how the markets, the economy, and geopolitics work. Yet at the same time it requires a certain humility, for you must recognize that no matter how good your information or understanding of current events is, you are going to make mistakes.

Fortunately, recent empirical studies demonstrate a simple technique that gives you an edge over other investors in consistently finding good stocks at reasonable or bargain prices. The next chapter reveals this remarkable "contrarian" strategy.

TEN

THE STRATEGY

"Dividends are probably the most maligned and ignored part of the average investment strategy."

THE MOTLEY FOOL

"The investor is more important than the investment."

DOUG FABIAN

Now we come to the practical side of *Investing in One Lesson*. How can we profit from the inherent weakness of investors who mistakenly treat investing like any other business, and who frequently overpay for good growth companies? We have already seen that investors and analysts, being largely short-term oriented, push the price of stocks far above what their fundamentals justify. We have also learned that investors are entirely too optimistic about growth stocks and uninterested in stodgy old companies that quietly deliver year after year. As a result, higher P/E stocks are usually overvalued and produce lower returns, while boring, traditional companies with low P/Es are largely undervalued, allowing for higher returns.

How can we use this knowledge to make money in the market? Fortunately, there is a simple strategy. In my research, I have come across one small, peculiar class of stocks that is usually immune from fads and hot markets, and that therefore sells at reasonable multiples. These stocks represent less than 20 percent of all stocks that trade on the various exchanges. They are so neglected that they do not normally suffer from the "rocky marriage" described in Chapter 3. In this class of shares, price seldom moves away from value. The marriage almost always remains intact. How can you identify these specially valued stocks?

A Simple, Powerful Way to Identify Value

Fortunately, there is a simple shortcut to finding well-managed, successful firms without engaging in all the research investors normally go through to identify these companies. It's not perfect, but it's a great strategy for individuals who want an uncomplicated method of picking stocks. The strategy helps even beginning investors to identify a group of companies that are likely to grow while offering shares that are cheap or at least reasonably priced.

This strategy relieves you of worrying about time-consuming, sophisticated, fundamental analysis of factors like earnings potential, cost accounting, executive compensation, cash flow, debt ratios, or stock options. You can ignore convoluted account concepts such as "return on investment" and the "price-earnings growth ratio." You don't have to pour over ten years of company statistics and current company reports. You can forget about interviewing customers, suppliers, and company officials to study their products and management skills. In his classic work, *Common Stocks and Uncommon Profits*, Philip Fisher highlights fifteen points—fifteen!—to help judge what stocks to buy. My strategy consists of one point.

At the same time, you have a very good chance of beating the indexes. It's vital that you have this kind of simple formula for investing. As Dick Fabian often said, "The investor is more important than the investment." If an investment strategy is too difficult to implement, it's useless to most investors. Keep it simple, and you have a practical strategy.

The genesis of my strategy can be found in Jeremy Siegel's comparison between IBM and Standard Oil discussed in the previous chapter. We noted that despite better growth data year after year, old-fashioned

Standard Oil earned a higher total return than the new economy stock IBM. What made the difference?

Dividends! IBM's market price was simply too high to overcome the gains from the hefty dividends that Standard Oil/Exxon paid out over the years. "Standard Oil's high dividend yield made a huge difference in boosting its return," declares Professor Siegel. Despite lower sales and earnings than IBM, Standard Oil's regular dividend checks made the difference in outperforming the giant tech company. Studies show that 97 percent of stock appreciation comes from dividends.

While IBM constantly strayed from its relative value due to overzealous investors who impatiently pushed its price up to above average levels, Standard Oil stayed true to its nature and provided steady profits to its shareholders.

There is growing evidence that companies that pay regular dividends show better long-term growth prospects and lower risk patterns than do non-dividend-paying growth companies. Because they tend to be large- and mid- market cap stocks that have been around for many years, dividend stocks are not normally subject to the extreme valuations that apply to new growth and technology companies. They stay married to their true values.

Dividend Weight vs. Market Capitalization

Moreover, you don't have to sacrifice profits to invest in dividend stocks. Recent academic studies find that stock indexes linked to dividends tend to outperform market cap index funds. *Smart Money* recently reported: "Independent research appears to back the fundamental indexers. Constructing portfolios based on earnings, dividends, sales, or book value going back five, ten, and twenty years across markets in the U.S., U.K., Europe, Southeast Asia, and Japan, a London research firm Style Research concluded that fundamental indexing outperformed cap weighted index funds an average 2-2.5% a year."

Jeremy Siegel's work indicates that dividend-weighted index funds beat market cap indexes by 300 basis points each year. That's a huge difference. See the following chart that shows the difference in total returns over a thirty year period.

LONG-RUN RETURNS OF DIVIDEND-WEIGHTED VS. MARKET-WEIGHTED STOCK INDEXES

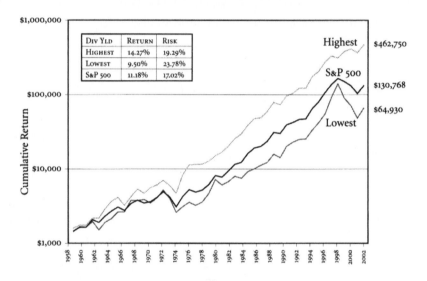

From the book *The Future for Investors: Why the Tried and the True Triumph Over the Bold and the New* by Jeremy Siegel. Copyright© 2005. Published by Crown Business. All rights reserved. Reprinted by special permission of Regnery Publishing Inc., Washington, D.C.

Show Me the Money

There are a number of reasons why dividend stocks are the single best investment technique for investors and comprise the "one strategy" I am recommending: **Dividends don't lie.**

A cash dividend is the only real evidence that a company is doing its job and that it's working for you, the shareholder, and not just for the company executives or its employees. In light of the many corporate scandals, questionable accounting schemes, and fictitious earnings reports of the recent past, there's nothing like a check in the mail or cash deposit in your brokerage account to assure you that a company is doing something right. It's comforting to know that a firm actually earned enough money to pay you, the shareholder. Cash dividends are not subject to revisions, like past earnings, which are always suspicious due to creative accounting. Revenues can be booked in one year or several years. Capital assets can be sold and listed as ordinary income. Liabilities can be written off as immediate income, or spread out over time. But cash paid into your account is a sure thing, a litmus test of the company's true earnings. It's tangible evidence of the firm's profitability. Admittedly, there have been a few dividend scandals, but they are extremely rare. It's not a financial trick or ponzi scheme. Dividends must be paid out of earnings. To quote the title of Geraldine Weiss's classic book, "Dividends Don't Lie."

Regular Dividend Payouts Provide Fiscal Discipline to a Company

It's similar to homeowners who must make enough money to pay the monthly mortgage. Or as Patrick Dorsey, head of stock analysis at Morningstar, states: "A company that pays a dividend is like an investor who commits to a 401k or savings plan—because the money isn't in your pocket, it can't be wasted elsewhere."

Dividend Stocks Beat the Market

As noted earlier, dividend-weighted indexes surpass market-weighted indexes by 300 basis points each year over the long run. A diversified portfolio of dividend stocks tends to outperform non-dividend stocks. Studies support this finding in international markets as well. In essence, dividends give investors the chance to buy stocks at attractive valuations.

Seldom do you find a high-flying stock that has a large market capitalization and pays a healthy dividend.

Dividend Stocks Are Less Risky

Studies show that not only do dividend stocks outperform non-dividend stocks, but they do so with less volatility. That's the nature of large cap stocks that pay regular dividends. By investing in these stable companies, you completely avoid the high-risk ventures of aggressive growth stocks, such as the tech bubble in the late 1990s. You avoid the Enrons or eToys of the future. At the same time, dividend stocks will rise in a bull market, though not as spectacularly as growth stocks. But it is during bear markets that they really shine. The dividend payout provides a cushion when growth stocks are crashing all around you; they are often a safe haven for speculators. That's not to say they won't decline in a bear market; they often do decline with the rest of the market, and they are not immune to the machinations of Federal Reserve policy and geopolitics. But they tend to hold up better than the hot stocks of the recent past.

Dividend stocks are good "go fishing" investments—they're dependable, relatively non-volatile stocks that are profitable to hold on to for many years. In the meantime, go fishing, enjoy life, and when it comes time for retirement, they'll be waiting there for you, most likely with a hefty return on your initial investment.

Dividend Stocks Provide a Great Way to Limit Your Investment Choices

One of the biggest headaches facing investors today is the myriad ways that exist to play the investment game. With over 9,000 mutual funds and 20,000 publicly traded stocks—and thousands more in the foreign arena—the choice of where to invest is mind boggling. Consequently, it's not unusual to see investors collect a hodgepodge of stocks and bonds in their brokerage account, with little rhyme or reason. Each stock or fund has its own origin—a broker tip, a newsletter recommendation, a "mad money" TV speculation, a money manager interview in a magazine. Instead of a portfolio that is well thought out, you end up with a chaotic zoo of unrelated investments.

But now you have a systemic approach. The next time somebody touts a hot stock or fund, all you have to ask is: "How much does it pay in cash dividends?" If the answer is "nothing" or "very little," you can safely answer: "Not interested," and look elsewhere for investment opportunities.

If you bought this book to find the next hot sector or the top ranked mutual fund of the past three months, you bought the wrong book. It won't turn you on to the next big IPO, penny share, small cap growth stock, private placement, emerging biotech story, or all the various funds associated with these non-dividend paying stocks. By limiting yourself solely to dividend paying stocks, you will avoid these kinds of speculations. This strategy could even keep you from throwing money away in some harebrained scheme touted by your brother-in-law.

At the same time, you do have a genuine variety of investment choices, including large-cap and medium-cap stocks, real estate development trusts (REITs), foreign stocks, Canadian income trusts, and a few commodity and energy stocks. See the next chapter for details and specific recommendations.

Responding to the Critics of the Dividend Strategy

Over the years, many analysts and commentators have argued against companies paying dividends. Here are the arguments and my response:

Argument #1: Missing out on spectacular early stage winners

Criticism: If you wait to buy a growth company until it begins paying dividends, you miss out on its most profitable history. For example,

Microsoft rose more than twenty-five-fold before it finally paid its first dividend in 2003, and has been a slow performer since then.

Response: The dividend method of selecting stocks definitely precludes you from profiting from the "ten baggers" favored by Peter Lynch and other financial advisors. Almost all the big stories of the technology revolution grew rapidly both in earnings and stock performance before paying out cash dividends. These include Microsoft, Applied Materials, Dell, Cisco Systems, Amazon, eBay, and Yahoo. Yahoo, whose story we discussed earlier in this book, has yet to pay a dividend.

Of course, there are a few exceptions. Intel, for example, has performed very well since 1992, when it paid its first, tiny dividend.

But there's a hidden benefit to limiting yourself to dividend-paying stocks: you avoid a high percentage of technology and other firms whose stock prices express irrational exuberance about their future—the ones that tend to go bust. And there are far more of them than there are big success stories that have survived and prospered in the new global economy. It is difficult indeed to predict a future Microsoft without engaging in a tremendous amount of research and getting incredibly lucky.

What about new issues or IPOs? They should be avoided in almost all cases. A Forbes report confirmed that after two years, the vast majority of IPOs sell for less than their IPO price. As Benjamin Graham wrote in *The Intelligent Investor*, "Some of these new issues may prove excellent buys—a few years later, when nobody wants them and they can be had at a small fraction of their true worth."

Other studies have shown that for every big IPO winner there are a lot of losers; the average IPO fails to keep up with the small cap indexes and is far more volatile to boot. Why is this? Recall my discussion of the "burning match." IPOs are priced to maximize the return of insiders, investment bankers, brokerage firms, and privileged clients. Unfortunately, they don't leave much money on the table for retailer investors.

It is not surprising that stockbrokers will often push IPOs on their clients. They have a financial incentive—a large commission—to sell you a new issue. So if a broker or financial writer urges one on you, tell him an emphatic "no."

Argument #2: Poorly managed dividend-paying companies

Criticism: If a company pays a dividend, it means it's a poorly managed company that can't decide a better use for the firm's funds. Companies that pay out regular dividends tend to be old, stodgy, slow-growth firms like the railroads that pay those dividends to bribe their shareholders to stay. However, a vibrant, growth-oriented firm needs every penny of retained earnings for its expansion plans. Most well-established companies (those listed in the S&P 500) used to pay big dividends, but now they know that paying a dividend is counterproductive to the company and its shareholders. Furthermore, high dividend payouts are probably a sign of trouble. Lower retained earnings mean less opportunity and are a sign of danger ahead for the company.

Response: In our previous discussion of the "Growth Trap," we pointed to studies demonstrating that the average return on older, slow-growth companies (including railroads) surpasses the returns of newer growth companies because of the difference in valuations and dividends.

Maintaining a high level of cash is no guarantee that growth companies will use their retained earnings productively. Companies with rapidly growing cash flows are often tempted to waste those funds on risky acquisitions or unsuccessful new products. In the late 1990s, for example, Cisco Systems sat on a huge cash hoard and instead of paying a dividend, spent the money on expensive acquisitions that eventually proved ineffective. Paying out a regular dividend puts pressure on the company to focus on projects that are more likely to succeed, because the worst thing that can happen to a company is to have to cut back or suspend its dividend. Imagine what that would do to the company's stock price or to the compensation to key executives, which these days often takes the form of publicly traded shares.

It's true that prior to the 1990s, major U.S. corporations were in the habit of paying healthy dividends, and the payout rate was over 50 percent. But in the "go-go" 1990s, the yield on the S&P 500 Index fell to under 2 percent, as more companies felt they could use the funds more effectively than by returning them to the shareholders. The 2000-03 bear market forced corporations to rethink this view, and dividend yields are now climbing again.

Argument #3: Double taxation

Criticism: Paying dividends should be discouraged because it amounts to double taxation. In the U.S., corporations pay taxes on their net income, which includes any dividends, and then individuals have to pay income taxes on the dividends they receive. By retaining their earnings, corporations do their shareholders a favor and pay them in higher stock prices rather than dividends.

Response: The United States taxes both corporate income and dividends, like most foreign countries do. (There are a few enviable exceptions, such as Australia, Mexico, the United Kingdom, and Hong Kong, along with many tiny tax havens such as the Bahamas and Bermuda.) This double taxation policy has indeed discouraged dividend stocks. Since 2003, however, the tax rate on dividends has been cut to a maximum of 15 percent in the United States. Responding to this tax relief, more U.S. companies are paying dividends.

This is not unusual—when taxes on dividends are lowered, companies tend to pay more dividends. For example, Australian companies pay average dividends of 4.1 percent—more than twice the U.S. dividend yield. Last year, Australian companies had a payout ratio of 62 percent. In other words, they paid out an average of 62 percent of their earnings in dividends. Why? Because in the 1980s, the Australian government eliminated the tax on dividends, effectively ending double taxation of corporate profits. In response, Australian investors began to demand more stock dividends.

The conventional wisdom is that high dividends mean slow earnings. But this is not necessarily the case. Between 2001 and 2006, firms in the Australian stock market (as measured by the MSCI Australia Index EWA) collectively grew earnings at a compounded annual rate of 19.1 percent, compared to 14.2 percent for firms in the S&P 500. There is no evidence of high dividend payouts resulting in slow earnings growth.

Argument #4: Warren Buffett doesn't believe in dividends

Criticism: Warren Buffett's investment company, Berkshire Hathaway, has never paid a dividend, and it's been a super performer. Shouldn't we follow Buffett's sound example?

Response: Over 70 percent of the top 1,000 stocks in the United States pay some kind of dividend. Buffett and his investment company have certainly been the exception to the rule. Over the decades, Berkshire Hathaway has achieved high returns from its capital and has retained all of its earnings. In 1985, Buffett asked his shareholders if they wished to be paid in dividends, and 88 percent preferred the existing policy. Lately, however, Berkshire's cash position has become so large that Buffett has admitted he's not sure where to invest it. The inevitable "law of diminishing returns" may well kick in at Berkshire Hathaway within the next few years—the company may get so big that it becomes difficult to find undervalued positions, for a company's stock price will shoot up as soon as Berkshire invests in it.

Argument #5: Companies cut or suspend dividends

Criticism: Paying dividends is no guarantee that companies will be profitable. Some dividend-paying companies have run into trouble and were forced to cut their dividends or have even gone bankrupt. For example, Ford's quarterly dividend reached 30 cents a share by 2001, but is now down to 5 cents a share. Even some companies in the Dow Jones Industrial Average, such as General Motors, cut or suspended their dividends after falling on hard times.

Response: Buying a portfolio of dividend stocks without examining the companies' financial condition will undoubtedly leave you with a few losers. Fortunately, however, troubled dividend-payers are relatively rare, being vastly outnumbered by distressed "growth" stocks. You are unlikely to run into trouble by investing in a diversified portfolio of dividend-paying companies, or in a fund of high-yielding stocks.

In 2007, the subprime lending scandal hit Wall Street, causing a collapse in the price of mortgage REITs that had a heavy position in subprime mortgages (mortgages extended to borrowers with below average credit ratings). Many mortgage companies foolishly lent money to new homebuyers who barely qualified and were unable to continue paying their mortgages once interest rates began rising. When they became delinquent on their mortgages, the high risk mortgage REITs fell out of bed, with many of them cutting or suspending their dividends. This example reinforces my recommendation to hold a well-diversified portfolio of high-yielding stocks. This will protect your portfolio from serious damage stemming from any single loss.

Argument #6: The efficient market theory

Criticism: According to the efficient market theory, it is impossible for anyone to predict or beat the market consistently over the long run, and dividend stocks are no exception. It's better to buy a diversified portfolio of 500 or 1,000 stocks and avoid trying to be selective based on dividends or anything else.

Response: The efficient market theory, which is similar to the "random walk" theory of investing, was developed in the 1960s by ivory-tower academicians, including three who won the Nobel Prize in Economics in 1990—Harry Markowitz, Merton Miller, and William Sharpe. Burton G. Malkiel, a professor of economics at Princeton University, sums up the efficient market theory as follows in his classic book, *A Random Walk Down Wall Street*:

It means that short-run changes in stock prices cannot be predicted. Investment advisory services, earnings predictions, and complicated chart patterns, are useless.... Taken to its logical extreme, it means that a blindfolded monkey throwing darts at a newspaper's financial pages could select a portfolio that would do just as well as one carefully selected by the experts.

Why can't professional money managers, Wall Street insiders, and individual investors beat the averages over the long run? According to efficient market theorists, the answer is competition. With over 100,000 security analysts in the United States and abroad, the market adjusts very quickly to new information. In this age of high technology and pecuniary gain, the rapid flow of information wipes out undervalued and overvalued situations within a short time period. This is what is meant by the term "efficient." Competition between market analysts make stock prices reflect their true worth.

Academicians point to many studies to support their case. For example, a recent study by *The Economist* magazine of the nation's top money managers concluded that nearly two out of every three professionally managed funds, measured cumulatively over the past fifteen years, have failed to perform as well as the Standard and Poor's 500 stock index. As business consultant Charles Ellis concludes, "The fact is that the investment managers are not beating the market. The market is beating them."

Efficient market proponents also point out that traders who buy and sell frequently have several factors working against them, including capital gains and income taxes, as well as transaction costs such as brokerage commissions, management, and bid-ask spreads (although recently these transaction costs have fallen dramatically as the markets have become more efficient).

Needless to say, brokers and security analysts reacted negatively to these initial studies, arguing that many individual investors and professional money managers, including Warren Buffett and Peter Lynch, have beaten the market for many years. Corporate insiders and floor traders on major exchanges are also known to beat the average investor consistently. Efficient market proponents respond by noting that mathematically, only a minority can beat the market each year; it is impossible for everyone to beat the market because, as noted earlier, everyone is the market. While admitting that a few superior investors beat the market for many years, efficient market advocates suggest that even their remarkable returns may be due more to luck than brilliant investing.

I've seen some evidence in support of the efficient marketers in this regard. For over thirty years, *Forbes* magazine has put out an annual Honor Roll of the best fund managers. While some fund managers have been able to stay on the Honor Roll for several years running, not a single manager on the list today was on the Honor Roll fifteen years ago.

Yet, I have pointed out time and again how often stock prices fail to reflect the fundamental and economic realities due to the peculiarity of human nature. As a result, there are anomies such as the dividend class of stocks that have consistently outperformed non-dividend paying securities.

What about Stock Dividends or Stock Repurchase Plans?

Sometimes instead of paying a cash dividend, publicly traded firms pay a stock dividend or announce a stock repurchase plan where they retire a certain amount of stock. Is this the same as a cash dividend? Not necessarily. A company that does not turn a profit can still issue stock dividends—they simply dilute the total number of shares outstanding while doing nothing for the bottom line or total investment return.

A stock repurchase plan, on the surface, is often viewed favorably by investors. It demonstrates that management is confident the shares are undervalued. And a buyback can make a stock look attractive by giving an immediate boost to earnings per share simply by spreading profits over a fewer number of shares. Recently, blue-chip companies such as

General Electric, Exxon, and Citigroup have bought back millions of shares. It's a growing trend.

However, a buyback program is no guarantee of investment performance. According to Birinyi Associates, a research firm in Westport, Connecticut, companies that had buybacks outperformed those that didn't by a mere percentage point from 2000 to 2005. The problem is that at the same time companies buy back their shares, they often issue more shares as compensation to executives and employees.

Share buybacks often represent nothing more than a feeble attempt to offset the dilution that occurs when senior executives exercise their options—they buy shares at a huge discount to the market, then immediately sell them. In the end, the number of shares remains unchanged.

The *New York Times* recently reported that two professors at Georgetown found "in a study of more than 7,000 buyback announcements from 1981 to 1995 that the number of shares in the companies making the announcements actually *increased* by 24 percent, on average." In the end, it makes no difference how big a buyback is if there are more shares outstanding in the end. Moreover, to add insult to injury, companies are not even required to follow through on their buyback announcements. The financing or cash flow may not be available. In sum, don't be deceived by stock buybacks.

Should You Reinvest Your Dividends?

When you buy a dividend-paying stock, should you instruct your stockbroker to pay out the dividend in cash, or should it be reinvested in additional shares? I know investors who use both methods. By automatically reinvesting your dividends in additional shares—the most common practice—you benefit from compounded returns. For example, it was the compounding effect of reinvested dividends that gave Standard Oil/Exxon its total return advantage over IBM. Remember, several institutional studies have shown that compounded dividend returns represent 97 percent of the total return on stocks over the past one hundred years.

On the other hand, you may choose to take your dividends in cash and use that money to diversify into other dividend stocks or funds. However, this requires that you actively investigate alternative investments. Some investors may not have the time or the inclination for such activism. My recommendation is to reinvest your dividends, especially if you are invested in a mutual fund or exchange traded fund (ETF).

Isn't Income Investing Only for Retirees?

Lastly, what kind of investor should buy dividend stocks and funds? The traditional view is that retirees and super wealthy investors should have their eye on income investing—buying large-cap dividend stocks in addition to government and corporate bonds. In contrast, young and middle-aged investors, with more time to achieve higher returns by taking greater risk, should focus on non-dividend growth stocks.

But the conventional wisdom is eroding. Dividend stocks and funds are good for all investors—young or old, rich or poor—because the returns are superior. Dividend stocks also offer benefits to various risk takers. High yield stocks may appeal to traditional savers who want their nest egg to grow, but want to sleep at night. Dividend growth stocks and rising dividend funds may be a good choice for conservative investors who want to invest in good companies without taking a lot of risk. And speculators may find a select variety of dividend-paying sectors with sufficient volatility and options attached to them to make them an exciting trading vehicle, including REITs, commodity stocks, business development companies (BDCs), and turnarounds.

While it is clear that dividend-paying stocks are a superior class of investments, the question remains as to which particular dividend-oriented stocks and funds are best, and what are their varying risks. This is the subject of the next chapter.

Eleven

MY FAVORITE INVESTMENT CHOICES

"Dividends are the critical factor giving the edge to most winning stocks in the long run."

JEREMY SIEGEL, *THE FUTURE FOR INVESTORS*

"Do you know the only thing that gives me pleasure? It is to see my dividends coming in."

JOHN D. ROCKEFELLER

What specific investment plans should you consider? Here are my "Golden Seven" stock market categories:

1. High dividend U.S. stocks, funds, and ETFs
2. High-yielding foreign stocks and funds
3. Rising dividend stocks and funds
4. High-yielding Dow stocks
5. Business development companies (BDCs)
6. Real estate investment trusts (REITs)
7. Energy and commodity stocks

I'm convinced that a well-diversified portfolio including all seven high-income investment areas—depending on your attitude toward risk—is the best way to build financial independence. Let's examine each approach in detail.

High Dividend U.S. Securities: Introducing Fundamental Valued ETFs

Exchange traded funds (ETFs), a new feature in the investment landscape, have many advantages over no-load mutual funds: they can be bought and sold throughout the trading day; they sell for close to their net asset value; and they don't make year-end taxable distributions. There are a variety of ETFs that pay dividends, but one group specializing in dividend-paying ETFs is WisdomTree Investments. WisdomTree has created numerous ETFs based on the work of Jeremy Siegel and legendary money manager Michael Steinhardt. WisdomTree's website states: "Our belief in the benefits of fundamentally weighted indexing led us to create a new family of stock indexes that define the dividend-paying segments of the U.S. and international markets. Our back tested research shows WisdomTree's fundamentally weighted dividend indexes generally would have outperformed comparable cap-weighted indexes, with less risk, during the long-term period tested." For a list of the company's current choices, go to www.wisdomtree.com.

One of my favorite ETFs is the WisdomTree Top 100 Dividend Fund (DTN). Rather than using a standard market-cap weighted stock index, it invests in the top 100 U.S. stocks with the highest dividend yield. As noted in Chapter Eight, this type of index has outperformed the market-cap stocks over the long run.

International Dividend-Paying Stocks

I also recommend investing in international stocks that pay regular dividends. Buying foreign stocks can be a great way to diversify your portfolio and reduce risk. Many top-flight companies in Europe, Asia, and other regions pay sizeable dividends, too. But there are important factors regarding risks and rewards to consider when investing overseas, a key one being currency. If major foreign currencies such as the euro and the yen increase against the dollar, American investors will benefit. But if the dollar rallies, a portfolio of foreign stocks will fall in value (assuming stock prices are stable in their own currencies).

Buying foreign stocks has never been easier, and many foreign stocks trade on U.S. exchanges as American Depository Receipts (ADRs). For easy diversification, I recommend a mutual fund or ETF in foreign stocks.

The WisdomTree International Dividend Top 100 (DOO) is an ETF that offers a great way to focus on dividend-rich international stocks. WisdomTree also offers regional high-dividend ETFs for Europe, Asia-Pacific, and Japan.

Liquidity is an important concern with regard to ETFs. So many new ETFs have been added to the exchanges that some only trade a few thousand shares a day. Fortunately, WisdomTree ETFs such as DTN and DOO are increasing in liquidity. Be sure to check how many shares trade on average each day to make sure the exchange can handle your order.

Rising Dividend Stocks and Funds

Hundreds of growth companies have adopted the best of both worlds: they retain enough earnings to grow, but pay out a cash dividend to their shareholders that increases each year. These are known as "dividend growth" companies. Studies have shown that companies that pay rising dividends are, in essence, showing their shareholders that they are determined to make money every year. The worse thing for them is to signal a lack of reliability in the company by lowering their dividend after years of raising it. Investors tend to dump stocks of companies that lower dividends—the share price usually falls by at least 30 percent. Furthermore, dividend growth stocks can be found in every industry—utilities, retailers, consumer stables, manufacturing, banks, pharmaceuticals, healthcare, and energy. Some companies have been increasing their annual dividend for half a century, such as 3M Company in St. Paul, Minnesota; Coca Cola in Atlanta, Georgia; and Colgate-Palmolive of New York, New York.

Since dividends have to come out of earnings, companies that adopt this strategy tend to start out conservatively—the payout ratio is typically 25 percent or less. But some large-cap blue chip stocks are paying out over 50 percent of earnings in dividends. The yield in dividend growth companies varies dramatically, from a low of 1 percent to over 10 percent, with most such companies paying around 2 to 3 percent.

Lowell Miller, who heads up the money management firm of Miller/Howard Investments, focuses entirely on the dividend growth strategy, which he calls "investing with peace of mind." His investment philosophy is based on the following formula:

HIGH QUALITY + HIGH YIELD + GROWTH OF YIELD = **HIGH TOTAL RETURN**

Miller believes that financially strong companies with rising dividends offer the most consistent performance and the highest added value. "Over the long-term, dividend-paying stocks outperform non-dividend paying stocks and companies that increase their dividends perform the best," he states. "Stock prices may fluctuate but dividends are always positive, and, over time, increases in dividends induce increases in the price of the equity generating those dividends." For more information on Miller's approach, visit his company's website at: www.mhinvest.com.

What's the best way to profit from rising dividends? You can either buy individual dividend growth stocks, or buy a rising dividend fund or

ETF. I prefer the easier approach of investing in ETFs. These are superior to rising dividend mutual funds, which pay a pitifully low yield of around 1 percent. For example, the Franklin Rising Dividend Fund (FRDPX), begun in 1987, pays less than 1 percent. Vanguard recently began the Vanguard Dividend Appreciation (VIG) fund, but it's too early to evaluate its yield and performance.

My favorite ETF is Morningstar's Dividend Leaders Fund (FDL). It's weighted toward mega-cap companies with above average growth potential that pay hefty dividends. I noticed that its top ten holdings are all rising dividend stocks. FDL has low volume, but is attracting interest. Its yield is 3.6 percent, and so far it's beaten the market with less volatility. Another good choice is PowerShares High Yield Dividend Achievers (PEY).

High-Yielding Dow Stocks

In the early 1990s, Michael O'Higgins and John Downs, two financial advisors, came up with an original investing strategy. In their book, *Beating the Dow*, they recommend that investors buy the Dow 10—the top ten high-yielding stocks in the Dow Jones Industrial Average— switching once a year to the new Dow 10. They dubbed their strategy the "Dogs of the Dow" because these stocks have typically declined significantly in price and are offering high dividends as compensation. Thus, the dog strategy is a crude way of being a contrarian by investing in big companies that are temporarily in trouble and could qualify as turnaround stories. Indeed, since 1973, the Dow 10 strategy has returned 17.7 percent vs. 11.9 percent for the Dow 30.

Another alternative is to buy the "Small Dogs," or what I call the "Flying Five" strategy. Here, you select the five lowest priced stocks from within the Dow 10. In my newsletter, *Forecasts & Strategies*, I've recommended this Flying Five strategy since 1991 with great success (14 percent annualized return, with only three down years). No system works every year, but this one has done well overall. For a list of the current Dow 10 or Dow 5 stocks, go to www.dogsofthedow.com.

Business Development Companies

Business development companies (BDCs) are composed of venture capitalists who finance private firms seeking cash to expand operations or to acquire other companies. BDCs make long-term loans and take equity positions in these enterprises, earning interest, fees, and share ownership in return. There are probably over a dozen BDCs in operation today, and most of them have been immensely successful. For income investors, BDCs have tremendous appeal because in addition to their long-term appreciation, they pay increasing dividends that often exceed 8 percent per year.

Allied Capital (ALD) is an excellent example of a successful BDC. Allied Capital finances a variety of mid-sized companies through long-term debt and equity positions and collateralized debt obligations. The stock has gone from $15 to $26 over the past ten years, while paying out an annual dividend of 8 to 9 percent. The firm has a rising dividend policy, with a payout exceeding 50 percent of its earnings. However, Allied Capital, like other BDCs, is not for the low-risk investor. BDCs tend to be more volatile than the market, but if you hold on for the long term, you should be richly rewarded.

American Capital Strategies (ACAS) is another well-managed BDC. It finances management and employee buyouts, provides capital directly to private and public companies, and offers senior debt, mezzanine, and equity financing for buyouts led by private equity firms. Since its August 1997 IPO, American Capital has invested approximately $10 billion in over 200 portfolio companies, including firms in services, transportation, construction, wholesale, retail, health care, and industrial, consumer, chemical, and food products. It has ten offices in the United States and Europe.

Since going public at $15 a share in 1997, American Capital has paid out over $22 per share in dividends. It has earned a remarkable 22 percent annualized return and a 500 percent total return over that time, assuming dividends are reinvested.

Venture capital financing has been good to me. In 1998, I decided to invest one of my individual retirement accounts (IRAs) in a limited partnership that finances natural resource companies in Canada. My IRA grew from $33,000 to $500,000—a fourteen-fold increase in nine years. How did the general partner—Global Resource Investments— accomplish this amazing feat? The president, Rick Rule, was constantly on the road or on the telephone, meeting and talking with company officials in natural resource businesses. He found the really good ones, financed these growth companies, took equity positions in them, and earned big returns through high interest loans and fees. Most importantly, he got in when these companies were cheap, before their stock prices took off in the recent commodity boom. And it paid off handsomely for him—and for me.

A similar venture capital operation founded by Rick Rule is now available through a publicly traded company called Quest Capital (QCC). Quest Capital provides bridge loans for promising ventures in mining, oil and gas, forestry, and water. In return, it receives low-priced stock and warrants when appropriate. More recently, Quest has financed real estate transactions in Canada. It only recently started paying a modest cash dividend (around 3 percent), but if all goes well, it should pay a lot more in the future. I recommend the company in my newsletter.

Real Estate Investment Trusts

Real estate investment trusts (REITs) are a popular way to invest in income-producing properties in the United States and around the world. They have special pass-through features for tax purposes. Most importantly, in order to qualify as a REIT, the investment company must distribute at least 90 percent of its taxable income to shareholders annually in the form of dividends.

In a broad sense, there are two kinds of REITs: equity REITs, which own residential and commercial properties from which they earn rental and fee income, and mortgage REITs, which finance the ownership of real estate properties. In general, equity REITs have greater upside potential to profit from rising property values, but they pay lower dividend rates (typically 3 to 5 percent). Mortgage REITs often pay double the dividend rates, with some paying double-digit yields. But mortgage REITs are also more risky, as evidenced by the 2007 subprime lending debacle. Investors would be wise to stay with quality issuers when it comes to the mortgage business.

Most of the REITs I've recommended in my newsletter have a rising dividend policy. They include the following top performers:

- General Growth Properties (GGP) owns and manages over 200 regional shopping malls in forty-four states. It has an excellent business model that immediately allows franchises to set up business in its shopping malls just by signing one agreement with General Growth Properties in Chicago.
- Hospitality Properties Trust (HPT) owns and leases 300 hotels in the United States and Canada, including Courtyard, Residence Inn, and TownePlace Suites by Marriott; Staybridge Suites by Holiday Inn; Candlewood Suites; AmeriSuites; and Prime Hotels and Resorts.
- Brandywine Realty Trust (BRT) develops and manages office and industrious properties in the United States.
- Centerline Holdings (CHC) is a financial company engaged in low-income tax credit housing, tax-exempt first mortgage revenue bonds, and multifamily mortgage loans.

- Municipal Mortgage & Equity (MMA) is known as MuniMae. It provides debt and equity financing to developers of multi-family and commercial properties in the United States. Most of its dividend is tax exempt.
- REIT mutual funds and ETFs are of the equity variety, and thus yield less than 5 percent a year. Most have enjoyed a good performance, though they are subject to interest rate fluctuations. If you want to invest in mortgage REITs, which are more sensitive to interest rates, you'll have to create your own portfolio.
- Equally, in real estate, the success of mortgage REITs depends on many factors—the condition of the real estate and mortgage markets, interest rates, the quality of the mortgage holders, and the management ability of the real estate investment company. You may be tempted to invest in a mortgage REIT that pays out a 15 percent annualized yield, only to discover a few months later that the REIT is forced to cut its dividend because of lower profits and higher costs. Buyer beware.

Energy and Commodity Stocks

Some readers may have heard an analyst on television or in a newsletter contend that the price of oil can't go down because "crude is a nonrenewable resource." This contention is supported by the Hubbert Peak theory, named after oil geologist Dr. M. King Hubbert, which holds that the amount of known oil reserves peaked in the 1970s. But this view is highly misleading for several reasons. First, while world production of crude oil has indeed peaked, known reserves continue to increase as new oil fields are found. Second, higher prices can encourage an increase in current oil production, especially the expansion of marginal oil wells. Third, higher prices promote the search for alternative energy resources such as tar sands, coal, dams, fuel cells, and nuclear power.

And fourth, higher oil prices motivate inventive entrepreneurs to develop more efficient uses of energy resources. For example, today automobiles and appliances use half the amount of energy that they used twenty years ago. As a result of all these choices, oil prices are not limited to increases only; prices can decline, and often have after an energy crisis.

A great way to profit from the energy sector is to invest in Canadian Oil & Gas Trusts. Thanks to rising energy prices these trusts have been especially attractive since 2000, boasting annualized dividends of 8 to12 percent, paid monthly. Canadian energy trusts earn their distributions from the royalties collected on oil and natural gas pumped out of their reserves. Since the pumping volumes are relatively constant, the royalties collected on existing resources vary mostly with oil and natural gas prices. If oil and gas prices rise, so will royalties and the price of these trusts. But if oil prices drop, expect the Canadian trust prices to decline also—and if they fall sufficiently, the trusts may be forced to cut their dividend.

The high double-digit dividends on Canadian energy trusts are deceptive. In most cases, they represent a combination of earnings and return on capital. The only way the trusts are able to maintain these high dividends is through either higher oil prices or by acquiring more reserves. Therefore, don't be surprised to see Canadian trusts cutting their dividends over time as new reserves reach their limit.

I recommend several Canadian oil & gas trusts that trade on either the New York Stock Exchange or the American Exchange, including Enerplus Resources Fund (ERF), Harvest Energy (HTE), Pengrowth Energy Trust (PGH), and Provident Energy Trust (PVX). While varying dramatically in price, expect all these energy plays to pay big dividends.

As for commodities, the choices are slim, for only a few mining companies pay regular, sizeable dividends. Take gold stocks, for example. Gold stocks paid dividends into the 1970s because there was no expectation that the gold price would go up; we were on the gold standard and the price of gold was fixed at $35 an ounce. But once the gold price started shooting up after the United States abandoned the gold standard in 1971, gold stocks were viewed as a leveraged way to play the future price of gold, and dividend yields declined sharply. The South African gold mines continued to pay high income, with dividend yields exceeding 10 percent, but they had a short life span. Those days are long gone. South African gold pays 1 percent dividend yields or less these days. Miners in United States are equally stingy, paying less than 1 percent.

Copper, aluminum, and other base metals provide a better source of relatively high dividends. Freeport McMoRan (FCX), with a current dividend yield of 2.1 percent, owns in Indonesia the world's largest producing copper/gold mine. Southern Copper (PCU) in Peru, the world's fifth largest copper mine, offers a rich dividend of 8 to 10 percent a year. Among blue chips, International Paper (IP) pays a 3 percent dividend, and Weyerhaeuser Co. (WY) pays out a 3.8 percent yield. Aluminum Corporation of China (ACH) is a relative new comer and pays an outstanding dividend exceeding 10 percent.

One popular no-load fund that invests internationally in energy and mining companies is U.S. Global Resources Fund (PSPFX). The fund has done well during the recent commodity bull market, but pays only a 1.7 percent dividend yield. Unfortunately, there are currently no well-diversified commodity funds or ETFs that emphasize dividend-only commodity stocks.

Commodities can be a good dividend earner, but investors must beware of the extreme volatility that we tend to see in the commodities markets. From a business perspective, keep in mind that raw commodities are found in the earliest stages of production. As such, their prices are inherently volatile compared to final consumer goods. Oil may double in price while gasoline prices at the pump may rise only 25 percent. Remember also that commodities are subject to speculation beyond normal supply and demand. Supply and demand may justify an oil price of $50 a barrel, but hedge traders and institutional money managers may bid up the price to $70 or $80 a barrel.

Commodity investing is ideal for the speculator who likes volatile markets. As the *Wall Street Journal* recently reported, "Commodities trading can be a brutal way to try to make money. Gains can soar by double-digit figures one month, only to fall the next." Most of the time prices are determined by fundamental supply and demand, and then all at once, "speculative fever" creates momentum in the market.

In general, the best time to buy commodities, especially gold and silver, is in the early stages of a rising inflationary environment. Gold is primarily an inflation hedge. When inflation is rising, buy gold and mining stocks. When inflation is falling, look out below. They won't fall to zero, like a bankrupt company, but they can fall 70 percent or more. I do not recommend a long-term "buy and hold" strategy on mining shares or commodity stocks. It makes no sense from a business valuation viewpoint. Better to play the cycle. Granted, the cycle can be long and can last for a decade or more. Just be prepared to take profits when the cycle turns against you.

Should You Supersize Your Income With Covered Call Options and the "Dividend Capture" Strategy?

Before closing out this chapter, let's discuss two strategies used by some funds that can double or even triple your dividend yield: writing covered call options and capturing dividends every two months.

The first technique has been around for years: writing call options on stocks you own, known as covered call options. Let's say, for example, that you bought one hundred shares of IBM at $100 per share. IBM currently pays a thirty-cent-per-share quarterly dividend, which amounts to a 1.2 percent yield ($1.20 a year). Suppose on December 21 you decide to sell a January $110 call option on IBM. This means that you have the right to sell one hundred shares of IBM stock at $110 per share between December 21 and the third week in January.

On the other side of the ledger, a buyer of your call option has the right to buy your one hundred shares at $110 during the same time period. The buyer pays you $200 for this right. You can pocket the $200 if the buyer doesn't call the option, and he's unlikely to do so unless the stock price rises above $110. If the option isn't called, you can add that $200 to your dividend, for a total income of $3.20 per share. Thus, by selling a covered call option, you earn 3.2 percent in income rather than the standard 1.2 percent.

What if IBM stock goes above $110? Then the option buyer may well call the stock on you, and you will be forced to sell your one hundred shares to him for $110 per share. But what's so bad about that? You now have a profit of $10 per share, plus any dividends you may have accumulated. This example shows why selling covered call options is often a good idea. The only drawback is that if the stock runs up on you way above $110 to, say, $150, then you don't realize the gain between $110 and $150.

The second strategy is called "dividend capture." Normally, if you buy individual stocks, you collect dividends every quarter, or four times a year. But some investors engage in a short-term trading system by trading stocks around their dividend dates. By holding stocks for only sixty-one days, they qualify for the 15 percent maximum tax rate on dividends. They buy the stocks two months before the dividend is expected to be paid, and then sell them right after the company pays out the cash. Thus, they can collect six dividends a year instead of four.

Several fund managers have gotten into the act. By adopting the "dividend capture" strategy, these funds can boost their dividend yield to 8 percent or more. Some open-end funds capture dividends in this way, as well as close-end funds such as Alpine Total Dynamic Fund (AOD), Eaton Vance Global Diversified Equity Income (EXG), and the Evergreen Global Dividend Opportunity Fund (EOD). But before you buy a close-end fund, see if it is selling at a premium or a discount to its net asset value. If it is selling above its NAV, wait before buying until the price falls to the NAV level. While you wait, the best choice in this sector is the Alpine Dynamic Dividend Fund (ADVDX), a no-load fund that has been using this technique since late 1983. I've recommended it in my newsletter, and it's currently yielding an outstanding 13 percent.

Keep in mind, however, that these "dividend capture" funds, as well as covered call option funds, are primarily for income seekers. Covered call options limit the upside potential of a company—you pick up extra income, but if the stock really advances, you have to sell your stock at a lower price. As for dividend capture strategies, they are short-term speculations for two months only, which means you get the dividend, but are unlikely to earn much of a capital gain. If you are looking for a "total return" investment, there are better opportunities elsewhere.

Twelve

CREATING A PERMANENT PORTFOLIO

> "A permanent portfolio should let you watch the evening news or read investment publications in total serenity. No actual or threatened event should trouble you, because you'll know that your portfolio is protected against it, whether it be inflation, deflation, recession, or war."
>
> HARRY BROWNE

> "Everyone is a disciplined, long-term investor until the market goes down."
>
> STEVE FORBES

A well-diversified portfolio consisting of the seven dividend-paying categories highlighted in Chapter 11 should serve you well. To repeat, these are:

1. High dividend U.S. stocks, funds, and ETFs.
2. High-yielding foreign stocks and funds.
3. Rising dividend stocks and funds.
4. High-yielding Dow stocks.
5. Business development companies (BDCs).
6. Real estate investment trusts (REITs).
7. Energy and commodity stocks.

What Kind of Investor Are You?

Before you decide how much you should invest in each category, you should determine what kind of investor you are. My experience suggests that there is no "one size fits all" investment ideal. Everyone has a different risk tolerance, depending on a person's philosophy, experience, knowledge, age, and net worth.

I've found that there are four basic kinds of investors:

Traditional savers

These investors seek to minimize their risks as much as possible by investing in extremely conservative investments where the principal is virtually guaranteed. Such individuals tend to invest in government securities; fixed annuities and other insurance products issued by large, safe insurance companies; certificates of deposit and savings accounts at well-known commercial banks; and money market funds. Traditional savers know little or nothing about the stock market. If you are a traditional saver and have read this far, you are probably ready to move into the second type of investors.

Conservative investors

Conservative investors are willing to take more risk than traditional savers in order to achieve a higher return. In addition to the traditional saving programs listed above, they will consider investing in blue chip stocks of large, publicly traded companies, some conservative A-rated bonds, and perhaps some well-secured real estate with positive cash flow. Conservative investors should limit their choice to categories 1 to 4, i.e., dividend-paying stocks, mutual funds, and ETFs; high yielding foreign stocks; rising dividend stocks and funds; and the Dow 10.

Speculators

Speculators are more adventuresome, searching for substantially higher returns that involve greater risk. All seven categories will appeal to the speculator. In particular, categories 5 to 7 (BDCs, REITs, and energy and commodity stocks) provide tremendous profit potential, volatility, and high dividends.

Aggressive speculators

Some speculators may wish to be even more aggressive. They may be interested in non-dividend secondary and junior stocks, new issues, leveraged mutual funds, hedge funds, foreign stocks and funds, precious metals, rare coins and other collectibles, and raw land and speculative real estate. Aggressive speculators will try their hand at fast-moving stock and commodity options, futures markets, penny stocks, highly leveraged real estate, and other unorthodox investment schemes. They tend to be short-term oriented, highly flexible, and willing to change their mind on a dime.

I've met all four types of investors, and they all have their strengths and weaknesses. The first two are defensive in their approach, seeking to protect what they have, and are content with getting rich slowly. The latter two tend to be more aggressive, seeking to risk much in order to gain profits quickly.

Know Your Limitations

One word of warning: it may be a mistake to attempt to speculate if you are by nature a conservative investor or traditional saver. Don't let greed or a charismatic financial guru tempt you into a speculative investment that you have no business entering. Even traditional financial planners often talk about the "investment pyramid" and suggest you put "some" (usually 10 to 15 percent) of your funds into more aggressive speculations. But I don't think this is appropriate for everyone. I remember well an elderly lady who had been a traditional saver all her life until the 1970s, when she heard a popular gold bug recommend she buy gold mining shares. Not knowing anything about the mining business, she ended up buying at the top. I recall her terrible anguish as she told me how she had taken her life savings out of a secure interest-bearing passbook savings account and invested them in a gold mutual fund, only to lose half her money. It was a sad tale of a traditional saver trying to be a speculator.

The more you know about investments and Wall Street, the more confident you can be in advancing from a conservative investor to an aggressive speculator. But don't try to be something you're not. It can only lead to trouble.

Take Advantage of Dollar-Cost Averaging Plans

Once you have decided your investment choices, you might want to consider setting up a dollar-cost averaging plan, also known as an automatic investment plan (AIP), with a major brokerage firm. (Go to www.markskousen.com for my current recommended brokerage firms.)

Here's how it works: Go to your favorite brokerage firm and ask for its AIP. While filling out the form, you will be asked to set aside a certain amount of money you wish to invest each month, and have this money automatically withdrawn from your bank checking account or regular paycheck. To keep it simple, let's suppose you agree to set aside $1,000 a month for your AIP.

Next, you select several dividend-paying mutual funds or ETFs to invest in each month. Five is a good number to achieve global diversification, and to keep it simple, you may want to invest an equal amount, or 20 percent, in each fund. But you will decide the best allocation based on your own investment philosophy and needs. Not all of the Golden Seven categories have funds that qualify for the AIPs, so you may be limited to only a few types, or you may have to instruct your broker to buy certain dividend stocks on a specific day of each month or quarter.

Three Reasons Why Your Portfolio Will Grow

Once you set up an AIP or dollar-cost averaging plan, you will be amazed how fast your account will grow. There are three reasons for the fast growth:

First, you are adding money to your brokerage account each month automatically, like clockwork. This is a great "forced savings" program. Because you have signed up for this account, you do not have to make the decision to save each month.

Second, all dividends, capital gains, and distributions are reinvested automatically, increasing the value of your account.

Third, if you pick the right stock indexes, the value of your account will add to your growth.

To demonstrate how fast your AIP account can grow by adding $1,000 a month, here are the results after various time intervals, assuming you average a traditional 10 percent annualized return for stocks, and that you reinvest all dividends and capital gains:

> After 5 years, **$60,000** turns into **$78,082**
> After 10 years, **$120,000** turns into **$206,552**
> After 15 years, **$180,000** turns into **$417,924**
> After 20 years, **$240,000** turns into **$765,697**
> After 25 years, **$300,000** turns into **$1,337,890**
> After 30 years, **$360,000** turns into **$2,279,325**

Amazing, isn't it? Of course, remember that this assumes a 10 percent annual return each year, which may not always happen. But with these three principles always working for you—regular saving, growth, and compounding—it's simply incredible what can be achieved by investing $1,000 a month.

These three principles of AIPs are the same used by investment clubs around the world: invest regularly, buy growth stocks, and reinvest all dividends and capital gains. Investors who follow this advice are bound to become wealthy. This is the essential message of George Clason's popular financial guidebook, *The Richest Man in Babylon*: save and invest regularly.

AIPs and dollar-cost averaging plans are a great way to save for your retirement, your own or your children's education, buying a house, emergencies, holiday gifts, investments, or a much-needed vacation. I have personally used this system to build wealth for myself and my family (especially my children's education), and I am always amazed how quickly the account grows.

This is also a great way to fund your Individual Retirement Account (IRA) or company retirement account. Most allow you to choose between a variety of mutual funds. In addition, company retirement accounts have two additional benefits: tax-free compounding, and some form of matching program in which a company matches your annual contribution up to certain limits. Thus, your company retirement plan is bound to grow even faster than a typical AIP.

Dealing With a Broker

To whom should you entrust your money? Should you open an account with a full-service broker, a banker, or a discount broker?

Every investor must choose some kind of stockbroker. Sometimes it is a rewarding relationship, and other times costly and painful. I've had full service as wells as discount brokers, with both good and bad results. Both types have their pluses and minuses. On the plus side, full-time brokerage firms and commercial banks offer a personalized service—a broker you can call regularly, who will answer your questions, and who can make individual stock and fund recommendations based on his experience, knowledge, and company research. On the negative side, full-time brokers and bankers can talk you into a bad investment, not be available when you want them, churn your account (engaging in frequent and unnecessary trades to earn more commissions), or encourage you to invest in stocks or funds that may be more beneficial to them than to you. You may end up with one of those stockbrokers who "know the price of everything and the value of nothing," as Philip Fisher puts it (with credit to Oscar Wilde). One of the biggest headaches is closing an account and moving on to another broker, especially after you have developed a friendship with your broker.

Discount brokerage firms typically offer lower commissions and the freedom to make your investment decisions without being influenced by high-pressure sales people. Most discounters will not tell you what to buy or sell. You are on your own as a money manager, and you have nobody to blame but yourself if you make the wrong decision. I think this is the best way to go if you are comfortable making your own investment decisions. On the downside, discounters don't normally offer the in-depth research reports of a major brokerage firm. (However, this is no longer the problem it once was, as summaries of reports and all sorts of other information are readily available on the Internet.) Finally, if you are worried about your portfolio, nobody at a discount firm will tell you how to improve it. They may give you some options, but ultimately you must decide yourself whether to buy or sell.

Most of my brokerage accounts are with discounters. I especially like to trade online, making my own investment decisions and taking my chances. Studies show that individual investors do better than most money managers. I think this is due to the personal responsibility assumed by the independent investor. Remember, nobody is most interested in your money than you are. Self-interest is a powerful motivator in investment markets.

If you do go with a full-service broker, I urge you to choose someone with considerable experience. Look for a minimum track record of five years that includes a bear market, for a person learns more from his mistakes than from his successes. As Philip Fisher advised, "It would normally be foolhardy for anyone to entrust his savings to the skill of a so-called advisor who had less than five years experience."

Threats to Your Portfolio and Net Worth

What are the most dangerous threats to your portfolio of high income investments? The threats might include:

- Inflation (rising prices, loss of purchasing power)

- Deflation (falling prices that might hurt earnings of the companies you own)
- Recession (decline in real economic growth or GDP)
- War (geo-political instability, terrorist attacks, etc ...)

The Key to a Rising Stock Market:
Free Enterprise and Stable Government

These threats are ameliorated when an economy enjoys political and economic stability. There is nothing automatic about a long-term rising stock market like the one experienced in the United States and other industrial nations for many decades. Country indexes rise over long periods of history for one significant reason: the underlying economy is predicated on a free-enterprise system supported by a stable political system, the rule of law, relative peace, low taxes, a stable currency, and limited government. As Adam Smith, the father of market economics, once declared, "Little else is required to carry a state to the highest degree of opulence from the lowest level of barbarism, but peace, easy taxes, and a tolerable administration of justice."

War, hyperinflation, or an unstable government can disrupt the stock market and send it into a tailspin. Look at nations that have suffered long periods of instability, runaway inflation, and tyranny, and you will find very few long-term bull markets. In some cases, the stock market has become illiquid, depressed, or disappeared altogether. Many countries—from the USSR to Argentina—have suffered such a fate.

On the other hand, recent studies by the Fraser Institute and the Heritage Foundation have concluded that countries that increase the level of economic freedom tend to encourage bullish stock markets. As noted in Chapter 5, investors would be wise to check the political-economic status of any country that they choose to invest in for the long term.

How would a diversified portfolio of dividend funds hold up if "Mr. Market" went crazy and headed for a crash? It all depends on how you split up your investment choices. As previously noted, dividend stocks are not immune to bear markets. Although they can cushion a fall, even conservative companies can decline in price, and sometimes sharply. Generally speaking, risk and volatility increase as you move down the Golden Seven income categories.

If you are a conservative investor averse to taking risks, stick with the top four categories. In addition, you may wish to hold other income investments, such as bonds and money market funds, which may offer better protection in a market downturn.

When Should You Sell?

Should you sell if your dividend stocks turn south? Not if you are a conservative long-term investor. Remember the investors who tried to outsmart the Magellan Fund and ended up underperforming the market? That's the danger of trying to time the market. It's usually better to keep adding to your account when stock prices are down. When the market recovers, you'll be better off. Overall, I recommend a well-balanced, diversified portfolio to protect you instead of a buy-and-sell trading mentality.

What about stop orders? Some seasoned investors, such as J. Paul Getty, never bothered with stop orders. Jesse Livermore is famous for the refrain, "Buy right, sit tight." As Arnold Bernard further notes, "Most of the money that has been made in stocks has accrued to those who bought stocks of good quality and just sat on them."

Speculators are more versatile and may use stop orders as part of a market timing strategy, attempting to sell at the top and buy at the bottom. But such strategies are beyond the scope of this one lesson in investing.

What Kind of Permanent Portfolio?

Financial advisor Harry Browne created the permanent portfolio concept in the late 1970s, arguing that a balanced portfolio of stocks, bonds, cash, and gold would hold up well no matter what happened. "Stocks, bonds, gold, and cash combine to provide balance and safety, one that will do well in any economic environment," he stated.

Browne's strategy is to invest equally—25 percent in each category— in four investments: growth stocks, bonds, precious metals, and cash (T-bills or money market funds). I believe this approach gives too much weight to hard assets, such as gold and silver, which have been volatile. The Permanent Portfolio Fund, created originally by Harry Browne, has a similar mix: 25 percent precious metals (20 percent gold bullion, 5 percent silver bullion); 10 percent Swiss franc bonds yielding less than 2 percent; 15 percent real estate and natural resource stocks, both foreign and domestic; 15 percent aggressive growth stocks; and 35 percent in government securities, including T-bills. Since its inception in 1982, the Permanent Portfolio Fund has had an average return of 6.38 percent, only one percentage point higher than 3-month T-bills. In my judgment, that seems like a small return for taking considerably higher risk.

If you are a conservative investor, my recommendation is that you create your own "permanent" portfolio by choosing from the Golden Seven categories and incorporating your investments into an AIP or a dollar-cost averaging program with your broker. If you wish to maintain a further degree of stability, consider adding a bond fund, prime rate fund, or money market fund to your portfolio.

And if you are concerned that the world is headed for disaster, consider adding gold to your portfolio as disaster insurance. Buy a gold coin a month and squirrel it away in a safe deposit box or home safe.

An Excellent Way to Improve Your Stock-Picking Ability

If you are nervous about how successful your portfolio of dividend stocks and funds will be, consider creating a virtual portfolio. Marketocracy (www.marketocracy.com) offers this opportunity. The website allows you to refine your investing skills by conjuring a million dollar portfolio of stocks. Already over 50,000 individuals from around the world have created their own fund or portfolio, and many have proven to be successful investors. Marketocracy's computerized program will monitor your stocks and any changes you make to your portfolio, then rank your virtual returns against others. I highly recommend this approach. I've done it myself, and outperformed their top traders. It teaches you a lot about yourself and your strategy.

In addition to dividend-rich stocks, you may be interested in diversifying further into the bond market, rental properties, and other high income vehicles. That's the subject of our next chapter.

Thirteen

BONDS, REAL ESTATE, AND OTHER INCOME INVESTMENTS

"And renouncing illusions,
 Find peace and content,
 In that simplest, sublimest of truths—
 Six percent!"

NICHOLAS BIDDLE, PRESIDENT, SECOND BANK OF THE UNITED STATES

If dividend-paying stocks are a good idea, should you expand your horizons and consider other income-producing investments such as corporate and government bonds, prime rate funds, money market funds, and real estate?

Let's examine the pros and cons of each income investment more closely. In this chapter, we will look at:

1. Government bonds and bond funds
2. Corporate and "junk" bonds and bond funds
3. Prime rate funds
4. Income-producing real estate

Income-Seekers and the Debt Market

How about investing in bonds that pay interest income every six months, or a bond fund that pays high monthly income? Are bonds just as good as dividend stocks?

In reality, the bond business is quite different from the stock market. By nature, its upside potential is limited compared to stocks. As a business, bonds can only earn what they pay out. If you buy a bond at par and hold it to maturity, you cannot achieve capital gains. Your only gain is the income you earn on the semi-annual coupon, which historically has averaged much less than the average stock return. You can earn more by purchasing a bond below par and holding for a capital gain, but even then most investors look to stocks and other investments as a better vehicle for capital gains. Thus, bonds and other income vehicles are best suited for conservative investors seeking steady income and little or no capital gains.

Warren Buffett has commented on this fact in his comparison between stocks and bonds. In his 1984 shareholders' letter—his annual company reports have become famous for pithy hints for investors—he explained why after World War II he decided against investing in government bonds. He noted that in 1946-47, thirty-year government bonds were returning only 1 percent per year in interest.

"In effect, the buyers of these bonds at that time bought a 'business' that earned about 1 percent of 'book value' (and that, moreover, could never earn a dime more than 1 percent on book), and paid 100 cents on the dollar for that abominable business."

He went on to say that "if an investor had been business-minded enough to think in those terms—and that was the precise reality of the bargain struck—he would have laughed at the proposition and walked away. For, at the same time, businesses with excellent future prospects could have been bought at, or close to, book value while earning 10 percent, 12 percent, or 15 percent after-tax on book. Probably no business in America changed hands in 1946 at book value that the buyer believed lacked the ability to earn more than 1 percent on book. But investors with bond-buying habits eagerly made economic commitments throughout the years on just that basis."

He concluded that from a business perspective, it made no sense to invest in bonds and earn only 1 percent when you could invest in good companies' stocks and earn 10 to 15 percent. So for the next three decades, he invested in growth stocks. For those thirty years, the same low-yielding condition, though less extreme, existed for bonds. It was a smart move.

But then in the early 1980s Buffett took a second look at bonds. Income investments suddenly looked favorable to him from a business-valuation perspective. He noted that thirty-year government bonds were returning 12 to 14 percent a year. In fact, he bought some Washington State bonds that were returning an after-tax yield of 16.3 percent. He commented: "Only a relatively few businesses earn the 16.3 percent after tax on unrevealed capital that our bond investment does and those businesses, when available for purchase, sell at large premiums to that capital."

He asked the all-important businessman's question: How many businesses do you know guaranteed to return you 12 to 16 percent a year for the next thirty years? Not many. Consequently, Buffett decided it was time to buy bonds—and he was right. They were an excellent investment to hold for the next twenty years.

But then came 2003, when the Fed pushed short-term rates back down to 1 percent. Ten-year bonds yielded less than 5 percent. Buffett recognized that robust growth companies could do a lot better than "safe" government securities. It was time to invest in the stock market again, both here and abroad. Not surprisingly, the stock market and Berkshire Hathaway (Buffett's investment company) continued to rise in price.

It's worth noting that in the entire post-World War II period, there was really only one time—in the early 1980s—when Buffett saw a good opportunity in bonds as a way to invest in a good business.

Why Corporations Issue Bonds

Let's look more closely at the nature of the bond or the debt market. Recall from Chapter 4 that corporations prefer to issue stock because it's the cheapest way to raise capital. Stocks don't normally pay dividends during the first years of expansion. But because the majority of individual investors are older and risk-averse, they prefer income investments. Corporations issue debt instruments to attract capital from these investors.

The debt market—including corporate, municipal, and federal government issues—has grown dramatically over the past decades. There are four major types of debt issuers:

1. Corporations
2. State and local governments (municipals)
3. U.S. Treasury securities
4. Federally sponsored credit agencies

Is the Debt Level Alarming?

Is the dramatic, almost hyperbolic, increase in private and public debt as bad as critics claim? Can debt continue to climb at such a rapid pace without ultimately making all of us pay the piper, ending in deflation and depression?

First, we need to understand the other side of the debt coin—the credit side. Creditors include savers, banks, corporations, venture capitalists, foreigners, investors, and institutions that lend money to the debtors. These individuals and institutions do not always want to take an equity position in the same capital-seeking enterprises.

They are in the business of lending money to borrowers after carefully considering the borrowers' credit-worthiness. In general, lending and borrowing money is an essential characteristic of the capitalist system. Of course, there will always be debtors who can't pay back their loans and businesses that run into trouble. That's an unavoidable risk in a world where the future is uncertain.

When a country experiences economic growth, it means people and businesses earn more income, and therefore have more to save and invest—which means more debt. Savings and debt tend to move together as an economy expands. So increasing debt comes as a natural result of economic growth.

"Junk" Bonds vs. "Safe" Treasuries

The real concern should be the debt pyramid and the unstable role of government. If a government fails to live within its budget, it can get into the habit of wasteful spending and monstrous deficits. The U.S. Treasury market is by far the biggest debt market in the United States and the largest, most liquid debt market in the world. Because of its size, liquidity, and safety, it has an unfair advantage in the market place. The result is often an illiquid corporate and municipal bond market. Many municipal bonds do not trade daily or even weekly. To compete with U.S. Treasuries, private corporations often have to issue "junk" bonds paying extremely high rates just to attract investors.

What a tragedy! Investing in free enterprise takes a back seat to investing in "safe" big government. Yet corporate bonds and commercial paper put resources to use, helping to hire workers and fulfill consumer demands. But because they are competing against "safe" Treasury securities, they must sometimes pay 2 to 4 percentage points more than the government does to attract money. It doesn't help that many establishment financial publications warn people against private "junk" bonds in favor of "safe" U.S. Treasuries and savings bonds.

Meanwhile, government paper all too often represents mere wasteful consumption and a misallocation of resources, crowding out numerous private capital projects.

Moreover, as the engine of inflation, the federal government has fueled easy money followed by credit crunches, resulting in a frequent imbalance between investment and consumption. It has systematically stimulated an inflation-deflation boom-bust cycle throughout recent times. It has not been an easy task for business to survive and prosper in such a volatile climate, and many businesses, big and small, have suffered financially. A good number have been forced to borrow heavily in the short-term just to stave off bankruptcy.

How does the business of bond investing work? In general, bonds tend to be more stable than stocks because corporate bonds pay an interest coupon every six months and return the nominal principal at maturity (anywhere from three months to thirty years). Back in the gold standard days, railroad bonds matured in one-hundred years and were backed by gold. As a result, the railroads could issue bonds at very low interest rates, sometimes below 2 percent.

Bonds are also considered safer because creditors have priority over shareholders in case of bankruptcy.

How to Minimize Your Risks in Bonds

But those days of stability are long gone. Investing in bonds now carries its own set of risks, including the following:

Price inflation

What is the present value of a stream of payments over thirty years? What will the purchasing power be of a $1,000 bond thirty years from now? An average 7 percent inflation rate will double prices in ten years. Given the constant temptation to engage in "easy money," long-term bonds could be worth ten cents on the dollar by maturity. Gold-backed bonds would be ideal, but since they are not available, inflation-indexed bonds are your best choice.

Higher interest rates

Rising interest rates are another threat to your bond investments, because bond prices are inversely related to interest rates. If you sell before maturity, and interest rates go up, you will lose some of your original investment. A 1 percent rise in interest rates can cause bond prices to drop 10 percent or more. If you hold until maturity, you will receive back your original investment, minus the loss in purchasing power. Also note: if you invest in a bond mutual fund, where no maturity date exists on the fund, you will never get back some of your principal.

Default

There is always the possibility that the issuer will stop paying interest on the bonds, or delay payments if the issuer runs into financial trouble. An average 10 to 20 percent of so-called "junk" bonds default each year in the United States, depending on economic conditions. During the Great Depression of the 1930s, many municipalities went bankrupt, although 95 percent of them eventually paid off their bondholders. Investors should check safety ratings by Moody's Investors Service and Standard & Poor's to determine the risk-level of their bond investments. Using a bond fund is a good way to diversify and spread your risk.

Most bond holders keep their bonds to maturity. That's generally a good idea, since they are particularly illiquid, with the exception of Treasury securities.

The gulf between private and public debt does have one benefit. It turns out that corporate debt, especially "junk" bonds, offers more opportunity to profit for investors willing to take greater risk. Studies by Jeremy Siegel and others have shown that the high-yielding "junk" bond market, taken as a whole, is more profitable over the long run than "safe" Treasuries. They are more volatile, and a small percentage default each year, but an investor who buys a diversified portfolio of high-yielding "junk" bonds and holds over the long term is likely to earn more money than an investor in government securities. The best way to do this is to buy a "junk" bond fund, which gives you liquidity if you need to sell. But again, your upside is limited compared to dividend-paying stocks.

Alternative Income Investments and "Crisis Investing"

In today's world, more investors are seeking alternatives to the traditional bond market in order to earn a higher income. I mentioned my favorite high-income alternatives in Chapter 11: equity or mortgage REITs, Canadian oil and gas trusts, commodity stocks that pay high dividends, and business development companies.

Like all equities that pay above-average interest or dividends, alternative income investments are subject to violent fluctuations, depending on geo-political events, fads, central bank policy, and the financial performance of the underlying company. To maximize your profits and minimize risks, it's best to buy after a sharp sell off. "Crisis investing" is my approach in this alternative income area. Buy after a major sell off, which can occur for a variety of reasons. In the late 1980s, for example, the U.S. government required savings institutions to eliminate "junk" or high-yielding bonds from their portfolios. Junk bonds collapsed, offering an incredible buying opportunity in the early 1990s to pick up bonds that were yielding in some cases 20 percent or more. Those of us who bought saw unprecedented high income plus capital gains over the next few years.

I also recommend that you learn as much as possible about the details of how each investment operates. For example, Canadian oil and gas trusts may pay high double-digit dividends, but in most cases, these payouts involve a return of capital, and are not comprised entirely of dividends paid out of earnings. Thus energy stocks are notoriously volatile. When oil and natural gas prices fall, the Canadian oil and gas trusts will decline sharply. When oil and gas prices climb, the Canadian trusts will zoom ahead.

Why Real Estate Can Be a Great Investment

Real estate in general is an excellent method of diversification, and I strongly recommend it for all investors and business owners. Almost every successful investor I know owns his own home, perhaps a vacation or second home, and maybe a few income properties as well. Running your own business is the number one source of wealth creation in this country, but real estate probably comes in second. The number of people on the *Forbes* 400 who have made their fortunes in real estate confirms it. Many individuals have started from scratch and become millionaires by investing in income-producing property. A friend of mine known for investing full-time in penny mining stocks has probably made more money in his real estate holdings around the world. In fact, I know a number of investment gurus who have been bailed out of bad investments by their real estate. In my own case, even though I have done well in most investment markets, my real estate has proven to be extremely profitable in almost every case, even though I have often bought at the top of the real estate cycle.

As soon as you build up some savings and retained earnings from your job or business, it would be a smart thing to buy a house or a rental property. It will pay dividends for the rest of your life.

Why is real estate usually a great investment? First and foremost, it an excellent "forced savings" plan. Real estate expert Jack Miller once said, "Want to make a million dollars? Borrow a million dollars and pay it off." He was referring of course to taking out a million-dollar mortgage, buying a house, and paying off the mortgage over a thirty-year period. Even if you run into financial troubles, the last thing you want to do is to default on your mortgage. Yes, it happens, but not very often, especially if you have a well-paying job. It's not unlike the automatic investment plan discussed in Chapter 12. And speaking of AIPs, they serve as an excellent way to build up funds for the down payment on a house.

Even if the value of your house only keeps up with inflation, you will gradually build up equity over the years because of your "forced savings" plan. Historically, residential housing in particular has kept ahead of the cost of living in most areas of the country and in politically stable parts of the world. Commercial building, however, tends to be more volatile.

The Risks of Real Estate Investing

This is not to say that real estate is always a "sure deal." Like the stock market, it is subject to cycles, risks, and to speculative fever during the boom times. Prices can fall as well as rise, and often do. Both supply and demand, including speculative demand, can increase and decrease in real estate. One of the biggest fallacies of investing is that real estate prices can only go up, or in the words of Will Rogers, "Invest in land because they aren't making any more of it."

Recall our earlier discussion showing that prices are determined at the margin. Property values, like the prices of stocks or any other asset, are also determined by a marginal number of buyers and sellers. All it takes for a rising market to turn negative is for sellers to outnumber buyers, so that sellers have to reduce their prices in order to entice more bids.

Look at it this way: Suppose the average price of a home in your neighborhood is $200,000. Who determines that price? The appraiser, you say. Actually, the appraisal is based in large measure on the price paid by sellers of comparable homes in the recent past. The number of homes sold in your area may number only a few during the past year. In most areas, no more than 10 percent of all homes are sold during the year. Thus, the only reason you can get $200,000 for your home is because most of your neighbors aren't selling. If they were, you might only get $100,000. When the market becomes glutted, you could face an illiquid market for a few years.

In real estate, the supply is not actually fixed or limited. Granted, a community may have reached the saturation point in terms of housing. The physical number of single-family houses and apartments may be fixed. But prices are determined by the number of properties actually for sale in the neighborhood, which is always a small percentage of the total properties, maybe 5 to 10 percent at any one time. And that percentage can increase or decrease. It's really no different than the stock market, where the number of outstanding shares is also limited, but the smaller trading volume—which establishes the prices—can rise or fall, sometimes dramatically.

For example, suppose real estate in New York City is really hot, and everybody wants to invest in the world's greatest financial center. As prices skyrocket, more and more owners in New York City will be tempted to cash out and take advantage of the high prices. Thus the supply of New York City apartments and condos for sale will increase.

Demand is another factor, even if the supply of salable real estate is relatively stable. If New York City faced some new threat—a terrorist attack, a natural disaster, an increase in crime, a large jump in taxes, etc.—demand for New York real estate might decline, and prices with it.

Just like any other investment, you must beware of speculative fever in real estate. If you are fully invested and fully mortgaged, and the market turns downward, you could be in for a rough time—and even the possibility of a temporary default on your mortgage payments.

Finally, there is the liquidity factor. So far no one has developed a way to trade real estate quickly, including the time it takes to close a real estate deal and pay all the taxes and lawyers. A house may sell quickly or take months to close due to market conditions, contingencies, and financial setbacks. High closing costs may also be a factor. The stock market does offer liquidity in real estate through REITs, but liquidity has not been extended to people's individual housing. Prices may not decline as sharply as they do with stocks in a bear market, but real estate can sit on the market for months, sometimes years, before selling. Sometimes in investing, you choose your poison.

What about Rental Properties?

I've always found real estate investing a fascinating field, full of would-be millionaires who are searching for a bargain property, a fixer-upper, or a hot market. My favorite book on the subject is an old classic by Bill Nickerson called *How I Turned $1,000 into Five Million in Real Estate — in My Spare Time*. My father, who loved income properties as an investment, had the original copy. There are many ways to climb a mountain, and real estate investing is one of the best. Just keep in mind that the more you know about the industry, including its often-overlooked risks, the better chance you have to prosper.

Many so-called real estate gurus guarantee overnight profits with "nothing down," in fact promising far more than they can deliver. I've never met a more consistent money maker than John W. Schaub of Sarasota, Florida, whom I've known for thirty years. In his book, *Building Wealth One House at a Time*, John tells the story of a speculator who, after attending a "nothing down" seminar, immediately went out and bought one hundred houses, many of them with almost no money. But he made the fatal mistake of buying faster than he could find good tenants. Eventually, he sold most of the properties for little or no profit — during a bull market. Schaub's strategy is much more conservative: "Buy one, rent one, then and only then look for the next deal."

The two biggest challenges for property owners is finding good tenants and generating positive cash flow — what amounts to regular dividends in the housing market. John's technique for finding long-term tenants is to offer a discount on the rent if the tenants pay on time, and another discount if they don't call for emergencies or repairs. He has had over 300 tenants over the years and only six have been bad.

The biggest challenge in today's market is to find a rental property that earns positive cash flow. Ah, there's the rub! Schaub says you have to work hard to find these bargains, which he defines as homes selling for 10 percent or more below the market price. He looks for sellers who have a large equity position, have a strong need to sell, and are willing to finance themselves; they tend to offer the best terms. He avoids apartment complexes and office buildings, and focuses strictly on single-family homes, preferably three-bedroom, two-bath houses in middle-class neighborhoods.

Like J. Paul Getty, John Schaub believes in patience when it comes to investing in real estate. He warns against the speculator who looks for short-term profits, and tells many stories of investors who got out too early with small profits, only to see their properties continue to rise in price.

Fourteen

THE LESSON REDUX

"Get-rich-schemes just don't work. If they did, then everyone on the face of the earth would be millionaires....Don't misunderstand me. It is possible to make money—and a great deal of money—in the stock market. But it can't be done overnight or by haphazard buying and selling. The big profits go to the intelligent, careful and patient investor, not to the reckless and overeager speculator."

J. PAUL GETTY, *HOW TO BE RICH*

"I have heard many men talk intelligently, even brilliantly, about something—only to see them proven powerless when it comes to acting on what they believe."

BERNARD BARUCH, *MY OWN STORY* (1957)

To introduce the "one" lesson of investing, I began this book with a disturbing story of a retiree who was eminently successful in his career as a medical doctor only to see his entire net worth wiped out by a single bad decision to invest his hard-earned assets in a fraudulent scheme overseas. Whether he was motivated by greed or ignorance, I do not know, and it was no fun telling this new subscriber to my service that his hard-earned assets were gone forever and he needed to start over again.

We all know that our full-time business or career is the largest source of wealth in our lifetimes. After building a nest egg, how can you best preserve and increase your hard-earned surplus capital? The key is to understand the basics of the "business of investing" which, as we have seen, is often unrelated to the concrete business that lies behind the publicly traded stock.

There's more to the art of investing than treating it like a business, as if stocks are subject to all the usual rules of supply and demand that govern your average company. You have to know what kind of business Wall Street is, and as we have seen, it can be treacherous, unlike anything you've seen in the job market. The business of investing is not the same as investing in a business. "Mr. Market" is distinct from the companies that make up the market. A company's stock is far more volatile and risky than the underlying firm because every business owner and shareholder can sell all or part of his shares at any time. Margin buying or selling can affect major changes in market values, causing stocks to jump all over the place, often unrelated to their true economic value.

There are many variables that influence a share price. Company fundamentals determine the long-term value of a stock, but in the short term, which can vary from a day to several years, stock prices can rise or fall depending on fads, insider trading, economic and political events, recommendations by influential people, and other kinds of extraneous "noise."

The stock market is increasingly being used as a casino or gambling house, encouraged by day trading and technical charting programs. These tendencies can make investing more volatile and dangerous, at least in the short term. But I am opposed to the adoption of new government regulations or special taxation to reduce this phenomenon. Generally, a laissez-faire environment is best for investors, and such intervention could only backfire by making markets less liquid. Rules encouraging corporate transparency and competitive markets, adherence to a stable monetary policy, and the presence of a vigilant financial press comprise the best recipe for consistent market performance and investor satisfaction.

Be prepared to profit from this volatile marketplace by investing in undervalued and neglected companies. Ignore the hot tips or the financial gurus' latest speculative play in favor of a portfolio of dividend-paying stocks. You won't double your money overnight, but you will achieve your goals of financial success. It is what I call "sleep well" investing.

Seven Rules for Successful Investing Based on "The Lesson"

Here then, in short, is my overall advice to readers of this book:

1. Depend on your main source of income—your career or business—to finance your investments. Live frugally (as Seneca wrote, "economy is a great source of revenue"), and add to your investment and retirement accounts regularly, preferably with an AIP or dollar-cost averaging program.

2. Become educated about this specialized "business of investing." After reading this book, keep on learning, either by taking a class in investing at a local community college or adult education service, or become self-taught by reading investment books, financial magazines, and newsletters, and by attending investment conferences. Read about the lives and ideas of the great financial giants, both past and present. (See the list of recommended classics at the end of this book.)

3. Decide what kind of an investor you are: traditional saver, conservative investor, speculator, or aggressive speculator. Limit your investment choices to those that suit your natural disposition, and follow the advice outlined in this book.

4. Open an investment account with either a full-service or discount broker, depending on your temperament and willingness to make your own investment decisions. Discounters are more appropriate for independent investors.

5. Focus on buying good companies that pay steady dividends. Conservative investors—including individuals not interested in

adopting investing as a regular hobby—are strongly encouraged to set up a "permanent" portfolio of well-diversified, dividend-paying mutual funds or ETFs. Investors should limit themselves to dividend-rich domestic and international stocks and funds. Be sure to add regularly to your permanent portfolio.

6. If you chose to have your funds managed by a professional money manager, be sure to investigate him thoroughly and do not rely too heavily on any one manager or financial guru. Make sure your money manager has your best interests in mind and will implement your strategy of focusing on dividend-paying stocks and other income plays. Even when using the services of a pro, be your own money manager as much as possible.

7. If you are a speculator, look for bargain opportunities in high-dividend stocks, especially those with greater volatility, such as energy/commodity stocks, the Dow 10, the S&P 10, business development companies, and real estate development trusts.

What If I'm Wrong?

Throughout this book, I've made the case for investing in one class of securities that largely avoids becoming overvalued and that can provide an excellent way to achieve financial success in the stock market. But what if I'm wrong? What if dividend investing becomes too popular, and this class of investments becomes subject to some fad, resulting in overvaluation?

That is certainly a legitimate possibility. Fads do change, and a popular investment strategy one year may be replaced by a new one the next year. Who knows? There may come a time when dividend investing becomes all the rage and the public ignores non-dividend-paying growth stocks. If that happens, expect to see a revised edition of this book. But for now, the dividend strategy exists below the radar. You will be among a small minority of investors consistently earning good returns without having the time commitments of investing overwhelm your life.

Recently I read a book by a CNBC business news reporter who interviewed some sixty-five seasoned financial gurus on what was the "best investment advice" they had ever received. Those interviewed included Warren Buffett, Jim Cramer, Suze Orman, Steve Forbes, John Bogle, Bill Gross, Robert Kiyosaki, Donald Trump, Jim Rogers, and Larry Kudlow. While they offered a lot of sound advice—from "buy good companies, not fads" to "don't try to time the market"—only one, Bob Froehlich of Deutsche Asset Management, mentioned the superior advantage of investing in dividend-paying stocks. In short, I doubt if income investing is going to become a raging fad any time soon.

A Story That Pays Rich Dividends

Allow me to end with a story of an individual who followed the simple strategy outlined in this book. A woman I know was married for many years to a rich man. She had many outside interests, and expressed little concern over financial matters. Her wealthy husband gave her a generous monthly allowance, but otherwise, never bothered to tell his wife about his financial affairs. So one day it came as quite a shock when he died suddenly of a heart attack, leaving her with a large portfolio of stock certificates. Knowing little about the machinations of Wall Street, she decided to take a simple approach to managing her newly acquired assets. If the publicly traded company sent her a quarterly dividend check, she kept the stock. If a company didn't pay a dividend or stopped paying a dividend, she sold the stock, investing the proceeds in dividend-paying stocks. She ended up keeping half the stocks from her husband's estate. Over the next few years, she found her dividend income gradually increasing, more than enough to keep up with her expenses. She soon became a very wealthy woman, able to enjoy her twilight years in full financial security.

In sum, dividend rich is rich indeed.

GLOSSARY

American Depository Receipt (ADR). A negotiable certificate issued by a U.S. bank representing a specific number of shares of a foreign stock traded on a U.S. stock exchange. ADRs make it easier for Americans to invest in foreign companies.

"auction fever." A situation where bidders get emotionally caught in the auctioning of certain items and pay too much.

Austrian economists. Economists who follow the works of free-market economists Ludwig von Mises and Friedrich Hayek, who taught at the University of Vienna in the early twentieth century.

automatic investment plan (dollar cost averaging). A program of withdrawing a certain amount of funds from a bank account or payroll and investing that amount regularly in a group of stocks or mutual funds.

bear market. A prolonged period in which investment prices fall, accompanied by widespread pessimism. The bear, which hibernates during the winter, is an appropriate symbol of a depressed market.

behavioral economics. The study of the psychology of individual consumers, business people, and investors who are prone to make mistakes, and how they can minimize those mistakes.

blue-chip stock. A large publicly traded company that is considered financially sound.

bonds. A debt instrument issued by corporations and governments for a period of more than one year with the purpose of raising capital by borrowing.

book value. A company's common stock equity as it appears on a balance sheet, equal to total assets minus liabilities, preferred stock, and intangible assets such as goodwill. This is how much the company would have left over in assets if it went out of business immediately.

bull market. A prolonged period in which investment prices rise faster than their historical average. The bull, which is known for being aggressive and somewhat unpredictable, is an appropriate symbol of a booming market.

business development companies (BDCs). Companies that finance private firms and in return receive a fee, interest income, or equity position.

"buy and hold." An investment strategy in which stocks are bought and then held for a long period, regardless of the market's fluctuations.

capital gains. The amount by which an asset's selling price exceeds its initial purchase price. A realized capital gain is an investment that has been sold at a profit.

commodities. A physical substance such as food, grains, and metals that is interchangeable with another product of the same type, and which investors buy or sell, usually through futures contracts.

contrarian investing/bargain hunting. An approach by investors and security analysts that looks for oversold conditions and cheap companies compared to the market averages and historical patterns.

day traders. Speculators who buy and sell stocks daily or even hourly, usually online.

distribution. The payment of a dividend or capital gain. Mutual funds often pay out a taxable distribution near the end of the year.

dividend. A taxable payment declared by a company's board of directors and given to its shareholders out of the company's current or retained earnings, usually quarterly. Dividends are usually given as cash ("cash dividend"), but they can also take the form of stock ("stock dividend") or other property.

"Dogs of the Dow." A strategy of investing in ten stocks among the thirty Dow Jones Industrials that pay the highest dividends.

Dow Jones Industrial Average (DJIA). The most widely used indicator of the overall condition of the stock market, a price-weighted average of thirty actively traded blue chip stocks, primarily industrials. The thirty-stock index has been published by Dow Jones & Company since the beginning of the twentieth century.

earnings. Revenues minus cost of sales, operating expenses, and taxes, usually reported quarterly by publicly traded corporations.

earnings target. Profits of a publicly-traded company that security analysts expect to achieve in the next quarter or annual report.

easy money policy. A policy whereby the Federal Reserve lowers short-term interest rates and expands the growth of the money supply.

efficient market theory. The controversial theory that all market participants receive and act on all of the relevant information as soon as it becomes available. If this were strictly true, no investment strategy would be better than a coin toss. Followers of the efficient market theory argue in favor of buying an index of broadly based stocks. Also known as the "random walk" theory of investing.

emerging markets. Financial markets of developing countries, usually small markets with short operating histories, including many countries in Latin America, Asia, and former Eastern European bloc countries.

exchange traded fund (ETF). A fund that tracks an index, but can be traded like a stock on stock exchanges. ETFs always bundle together the securities that are in an index; they never track actively managed mutual fund portfolios.

"Flying Five" strategy. A strategy of investing in the five highest yielding, lowest priced Dow thirty stocks.

fundamentalist. In finance, a method of security valuation which involves examining the company's financials and operations, especially sales, earnings, growth potential, assets, debt, management, products, and competition.

futures. Standardized, transferable, exchange-traded contracts that require delivery of a commodity, bond, currency, or stock index at a specified price, on a specified future date. Unlike options, futures convey an obligation to buy. The risk to the holder is unlimited, and because the payoff pattern is symmetrical, the risk to the seller is unlimited as well. Dollars lost and gained by each party on a futures contract are equal and opposite.

GDP growth. Increase in Gross Domestic Product, the total value of final goods and services purchased by consumers, business, and government in one year.

"going public." Performing an initial public offering (IPO). Opposite of going private.

growth stocks. Stocks of a company that is growing earnings and/or revenue faster than its industry or the overall market. Such companies usually pay little or no dividends, preferring to use the income instead to finance further expansion.

hedge fund. A fund, usually used by wealthy individuals and institutions, that is allowed to use aggressive strategies that are unavailable to mutual funds, including selling short, leverage, program trading, swaps, arbitrage, and derivatives.

Hubbert Peak theory. Named after American geophysicist Marion King Hubbert, who predicted that the amount of oil under the ground is finite and has probably peaked in the United States.

illiquid. Not easily convertible to cash. Opposite of liquid.

incorporating a business. The process by which a business receives a state charter, allowing it to become a corporation.

index fund. A composition of stocks valued usually by market capitalization, such as the S&P 500 or Russell 2000.

Initial Public Offering (IPO). The first sale of stock by a company to the public.

junk bonds. A slang term for high-risk, non-investment-grade bonds with a low credit rating, usually BB or lower; as a consequence, they usually have a high yield. Opposite of investment-grade bonds.

leverage. The degree to which an investor or business is utilizing borrowed money. Companies that are highly leveraged may be at risk of bankruptcy if they are unable to make payments on their debt; they may also be unable to find new lenders in the future. Leverage is not always bad, however; it can increase the shareholders' return on their investment and there are often tax advantages associated with borrowing. Also called financial leverage.

liquid. Easily convertible to cash. Opposite of illiquid.

margin call. A call from a broker to a customer (called a maintenance margin call) demanding the deposit of cash or marginable securities in order to cover losses from an adverse price movement. A margin call is usually associated with the purchase of a stock or commodity on margin; that is, with borrowed money.

marginal behavior. Price action of an investment based on a small number of buyers and sellers.

market capitalization. The aggregate value of a company or stock. It is obtained by multiplying the number of shares outstanding by their current price per share.

market timing. Attempting to predict future market directions, usually by examining recent price and volume data or economic data, and investing based on those predictions. Also called timing the market.

market-weighted index. An index of stocks valued according to their market capitalization, such as the S&P 500 Index.

money market funds. Open-end mutual funds that invest only in money markets and operate like an interest-bearing checking account. These funds invest in short-term (one day to one year) debt obligations such as Treasury bills, certificates of deposit, and commercial paper. The main goal is the preservation of principal, accompanied by modest dividends.

mutual funds. Open-ended funds operated by an investment company that raise money from shareholders and invest in a group of assets in accordance with a stated set of objectives. Mutual funds raise money by selling shares of the fund to the public.

Nasdaq. A computerized system established by the National Association of Securities Dealers (NASD) to facilitate trading by providing broker/dealers with current bid and ask price quotes on over-the-counter stocks and some listed stocks. Unlike the Amex and the NYSE, the Nasdaq (once an acronym for the National Association of Securities Dealers Automated Quotation system) trades stocks over a network of computers and telephones.

New York Stock Exchange (NYSE). The oldest and largest stock exchange in the U.S., located on Wall Street in New York City. The NYSE is responsible for setting policy, supervising member activities, listing securities, overseeing the transfer of member seats, and evaluating applicants. It traces its origins back to 1792.

price-earnings ratio (P/E ratio). The most common measure of how expensive a stock is. The P/E ratio is equal to a stock's market capitalization divided by its after-tax earnings over a twelve-month period, usually the trailing period but occasionally the current or forward period.

prime rate fund. Mutual fund that attempts to match the return of the prime rate by investing in high-quality corporate debt. The prime rate is the interest rate a commercial bank charges its best corporate customers. Prime rate funds tend to increase their dividends when interest rates rise.

privately held company. A company whose shares are owned by individuals and institutions and do not trade on a publicly traded exchange.

profits. Gain from an investment or business operation after subtracting for all expenses. See also *earnings*.

publicly traded company. A company whose shares trade on an official exchange, such as the New York Stock Exchange or Nasdaq.

quarterly report. Unaudited document required by the SEC for all U.S. public companies, reporting the financial results for the quarter and noting any significant changes or events in the quarter. Quarterly reports contain financial statements, a discussion from the management, and a list of "material events" that have occurred with the company (such as a stock split or acquisition). Also called Form 10-Q.

real estate investment trust (REIT). A corporation or trust that uses the pooled capital of many investors to purchase and manage income property and/or mortgage loans.

"regression to the mean." In finance, this is the view held by many economists and financial analysts that the price of overvalued companies must eventually fall, and undervalued companies must rise to their intrinsic value.

REIT (equity). Real estate investment trust that takes an ownership position in its real estate investments, as opposed to a mortgage REIT.

REIT (mortgage). Real estate investment trust that invests in mortgages; some also borrow money from banks and re-lend it at higher interest rates.

returns. The annual return on an investment, expressed as a percentage of the total amount invested. Also called rate of return.

revenues. Total amount of money received by a company for goods sold or services provided, usually reported quarterly by publicly traded companies. Revenues also include sale of assets.

rising dividends. A company policy of paying a higher dividend over time.

Securities and Exchange Commission (SEC). Founded in 1933, the primary federal regulatory agency for the securities industry, whose responsibility is to promote full disclosure and to protect investors against fraudulent and manipulative practices in the securities markets.

shorting a stock. Borrowing a security (or commodity futures contract) from a broker and selling it, with the understanding that it must later be bought back (hopefully at a lower price) and returned to the broker. Short selling is a technique used by investors who try to profit from the falling price of a stock. Also called selling short.

speculator. An individual who takes large risks, especially with respect to trying to predict the future; a person who gambles in hopes of making quick, large gains.

Standard & Poor's 500 index (S&P 500). A basket of 500 stocks that are considered to be widely held. Created in 1957, the S&P 500 is weighted by market value, and its performance is thought to be representative of the stock market as a whole.

stock market bubble. A description of rapidly rising equity prices, usually in a particular sector, that some investors feel is unfounded. The term is used because, like a bubble, the prices will reach a point at which they pop and collapse violently.

stock option. The right, but not the obligation, to buy (for a call option) or sell (for a put option) a specific amount of a given stock, commodity, currency, index, or debt at a specified price (the strike price) during a specified period of time. For stock options, the amount is usually one hundred shares. Each option has a buyer, called the holder, and a seller, known as the writer. If the option contract is exercised, the writer is responsible for fulfilling the terms of the contract by delivering the shares to the appropriate party.

stock repurchase plan. A corporation's repurchase of stock it has issued, thus reducing the number of shares outstanding, giving each remaining shareholder a larger percentage ownership of the company.

stocks. Ownership in a corporation that represents a claim on its proportional share in the corporation's assets and profits. Also called equity.

subprime lender. A mortgage lender to a borrower who has below-average credit.

technical trader. A trader who uses a method of evaluating securities by relying on the assumption that market data, such as charts of price, volume, and open interest, can help predict future (usually short-term) market trends. Unlike fundamental analysis, the intrinsic value of the security is not considered.

tight money policy. A policy whereby the Federal Reserve raises short-term interest rates and reduces the growth of the money supply.

underwriter. A brokerage firm or investment banker who acts as an intermediary between an issuer of a security and the investing public in the release of an IPO.

U.S. Federal Reserve (The Fed). The seven-member Board of Governors that oversees Federal Reserve Banks, establishes monetary policy (interest rates, credit, etc.), and monitors the economic health of the country. Its members are appointed by the president, subject to Senate confirmation, and serve fourteen-year terms.

U.S. Treasuries. Short-and long-term debt issued by the United States government.

value stocks. Stocks that are considered to be good stocks at a great price based on their fundamentals, as opposed to great stocks at a good price. Generally, these stocks are contrasted with growth stocks that trade at high multiples to earnings and cash.

venture capitalist. An entrepreneur who helps other entrepreneurs financially and often plays an active role in the company's operations (for example, by occupying a seat on the board of directors).

volatility. The relative rate at which the price of a security moves up and down. Volatility is found by calculating the annualized standard deviation of the daily change in price. If the price of a stock moves up and down rapidly over short time periods, it has high volatility. If the price almost never changes, it has low volatility.

yield. The annual rate of return on an investment, expressed as a percentage.

RECOMMENDED BOOKS IN
INVESTING IN ONE LESSON

Barnard Baruch, *My Own Story*, 2 volumes (Holt, Rinehart and Winston, 1957, 1960).

George S. Clason, *The Richest Man in Babylon* (Penguin Books, 1926).

J. Paul Getty, *How to Be Rich* (Jove, 1965).

Benjamin Graham, *The Intelligent Investor* (Collins, 2003 [1949]).

Peter Lynch, *One Up on Wall Street* (Simon & Schuster, 2000).

Charles Mackay, *Extraordinary Popular Delusions and the Madness of Crowds* (Three Rivers Press, 1995 [1841]).

Burton Malkiel, *A Random Walk Down Wall Street* (Norton, 2004).

Humphrey O'Neill, *The Art of Contrary Thinking* (Caxton Press, 1997).

Fred Schwed, Jr., *Where are the Customers' Yachts?* (Wiley, 1995).

Jeremy J. Siegel, *The Future for Investors* (Crown Business, 2005).

All these books are still in print and are available in bookstores or on www.amazon.com.

ABOUT THE AUTHOR

Mark Skousen is a professional economist, financial advisor, university professor, and book author. Since 1980, Dr. Skousen has been editor in chief of *Forecasts & Strategies*, a popular award-winning investment newsletter published by Eagle Publishing in Washington, D. C. (available at www.markskousen.com). He is also editor of his own website, www.mskousen.com, and edits three trading services: Skousen Hedge Fund Trader, High Income Alert, and Turnaround Trader. From 2005 to 2007 he was chairman of Investment U (www.investmentu. com), one of the largest investment e-letters in the country, with over 300,000 subscribers. He now publishes his own e-mail letter, available at www.worldlyphilosophers.com

In 2004–05, Dr. Skousen taught economics and finance at Columbia Business School and Barnard College at Columbia University. In 2001–02, he was president of the Foundation of Economic Education (FEE) in New York. From 1986 until 2003, he taught economics, finance, and history at Rollins College in Winter Park, Florida. In honor of his work in economics, finance, and management, Gratham University renamed its business school "The Mark Skousen School of Business" in 2005, where he holds the Benjamin Franklin Chair in Management.

From 1972–75, Dr. Skousen was an economic analyst for the Central Intelligence Agency. Since then, he has been a consultant to IBM, Hutchinson Technology, and other Fortune 500 companies. He has been a columnist for *Forbes* magazine (1997-2001), and has written articles for the *Wall Street Journal*, *Liberty*, *Reason*, and the *Journal of*

Economic Perspectives. He has appeared on ABC News, CNBC *Power Lunch*, CNN, FOXNews, and C-SPAN Book TV.

Dr. Skousen earned his Ph. D. in economics and monetary history from George Washington University in 1977. Since then he has written over twenty books, including *The Structure of Production* (New York University Press, 1990), *Economics on Trial* (McGraw Hill, 1991), *Puzzles and Paradoxes in Economics* (Edward Elgar Publishers, 1997), *Economic Logic* (Capital Press, 2000), *The Making of Modern Economics* (M. E. Sharpe, 2001), *The Power of Economic Thinking* (Foundation for Economic Education, 2002), *Vienna and Chicago, Friends or Foes?* (Capital Press, 2005), *The Compleated Autobiography by Benjamin Franklin* (Regnery Publishing, 2006), and *The Big Three in Economics* (M. E. Sharpe, 2007).

His financial bestsellers include *The Complete Guide to Financial Privacy* (Simon & Schuster, 1983), *High Finance on a Low Budget* (Bantam, 1981), co-authored with his wife Jo Ann, and *Scrooge Investing* (Little Brown, 1995; McGraw Hill, 1999).

He was also editor of the investment series, "Secrets of the Great Investors," with Louis Rukeyser as narrator, now available from Blackstone Audio (www.blackstoneaudio.com).

Dr. Skousen has lived in eight nations, and traveled and lectured throughout the United States and in seventy countries. He grew up in Portland, Oregon. He, his wife Jo Ann, and their five children have lived in Washington, D.C.; Nassau, the Bahamas; London, England; Orlando, Florida; and New York.

Websites

www.mskousen.com
www.markskousen.com
www.worldlyphilosophers.com

Email address

editor@markskousen.com

MY INVESTMENT NEWSLETTER AND TRADING SERVICE

I offer two services to help investors improve upon the one lesson of investing and stay up-to-date on investment trends in general:

My Monthly Investment Newsletter

I've been writing *Forecasts & Strategies* since 1980. Published by Eagle Publishing in Washington, D.C., each issue begins with an overview of the economy, the Federal Reserve, interest rates, and geopolitics, explaining how these macro-economic events may impact your investments. The second half deals with specific investment recommendations in stocks, bonds, foreign markets, commodities, and real estate. Every issue has a special section on dividend-paying stocks and high-income investing. I also put out a voice hotline every Monday morning to update investors. The annual fee is $250 a year, but we have an introductory offer of $99.95 for the first year. To subscribe, go to www. markskousen.com, or call Eagle Publishing at (800) 211-7661 or (202) 216-0600.

My Trading Service

Skousen High Income Alert is a trading service focusing on special situations in high-dividend-paying stocks that are temporarily undervalued and offer tremendous upside potential. This is a short-term trading service, where we hold high-dividend stocks for less than six months. Over the years, I've discovered that stocks that pay above average yields are highly volatile and offer excellent trading vehicles for short-term profits. So far, the *Skousen High Income Alert* has been "highly" successful (excuse the pun), although future results, naturally, cannot be guaranteed. The service also offers optional stock option trading recommendations for aggressive speculators who wish to take greater risks for higher profit potential. The cost is $995 per year, or $295 per quarter. For more information, go to www.skousenhighincomealert.com, or call toll-free (800) 211-7661.

OTHER BOOKS
BY MARK SKOUSEN

The Complete Guide to Financial Privacy

High Finance on a Low Budget, co-authored with Jo Ann
Skousen

Tax Free

Scrooge Investing

The Making of Modern Economics

The Power of Economic Thinking

The Big Three in Economics

The Compleated Autobiography by Benjamin Franklin, compiler
and editor

ACKNOWLEDGMENTS

The lesson of this book is derived from the relatively new science of "behavioral economics," and I wish to thank in particular Jeremy Siegel at the Wharton School at the University of Pennsylvania, whose research has been invaluable, as well as Robert Shiller at Yale University and Richard Thaler at the University of Chicago. I've also relied on the advice of money manager Lowell Miller of Miller/Howard Investments and international tax attorney Marshall Langer, among others.

The title of this book comes from a book I've always been fond of, *Economics in One Lesson*, by Henry Hazlitt. I hope my book can measure up to this classic.

I've developed friendships with many experts in the financial field, and have learned many lessons from them. It would be impossible to list them all here. But I would like to mention in particular several giants in the field whose writings have influenced me: J. Paul Getty and his eighteen-page chapter "The Wall Street Investor" in *How to Be Rich*, the best single essay ever written on the stock market; George S. Clason, author of *The Richest Man in Babylon*, the most significant financial literary work ever penned; Benjamin Graham, author of *The Intelligent Investor*, who introduced me to maniac depressive "Mr. Market"; and other speculator kings such as Bernard Baruch, Arnold Bernard, John Templeton, Philip Fisher, and Jesse Livermore. Reading the memoirs of these giants of finance is always valuable and comforting.

I am also grateful to the many editors of financial newsletters I have met over the years; columnists for magazines and newspapers; economists and professors; authors; publishers and printers; presidents of companies, both large and small; government officials; stockbrokers and dealers in coins and other investment products; and thousands of subscribers whom I have met and befriended through my newsletter, *Forecasts & Strategies*. All of them have contributed to my understanding of the strange and often frustrating business of investing.

I would like to thank my publishers and editors at Regnery Publishing for supporting me in this project, as well as the anonymous referees who reviewed the manuscript and recommended some important changes. And most of all, I must convey my gratitude to my wife Jo Ann, my partner in writing, family, and life, who has been instrumental in transforming this book into a meaningful single message.

Be free, AEIOU,

Mark Skousen

INDEX